VERBAL JUDO

Publication Number 1062

AMERICAN LECTURE SERIES®

A Monograph in

The BANNERSTONE DIVISION of
AMERICAN LECTURES IN BEHAVIORAL SCIENCE AND LAW

Edited by

RALPH SLOVENKO, B.E., LL.B., M.A., Ph.D.
Professor of Law and Psychiatry
Wayne State University Law School
Detroit, Michigan

*Book 1 — looks new
granted*

VERBAL JUDO

WORDS AS A FORCE OPTION

By

GEORGE J. THOMPSON

President
Verbal Judo Institute, Inc.
Auburn, New York

Doc Rhino t.
1/4/10

CHARLES C THOMAS · PUBLISHER, LTD.
Springfield · Illinois · U.S.A.

Published and Distributed Throughout the World by
CHARLES C THOMAS • PUBLISHER
2600 South First Street
Springfield, Illinois 62717

© *1983 by* CHARLES C THOMAS • PUBLISHER
ISBN 978-0-398-04879-2 (hard)
ISBN 978-0-398-06456-3 (paper)
Library of Congress Catalog Card Number: 83-9164

With THOMAS BOOKS *careful attention is given to all details of manufacturing and*
design. It is the Publisher's desire to present books that are satisfactory as to their physical
qualities and artistic possibilities and appropriate for their particular use. THOMAS
BOOKS *will be true to those laws of quality that assure a good name and good will.*

Printed in the United States of America
Q-R-3

Library of Congress Cataloging in Publication Data
Thompson, George J.
    Verbal judo.

    (American lecture series. A monograph in the
Bannerstone Division of American lectures in behavioral
science and law ; no. 1062)
    Bibliography: p.
    Includes index.
    1. Interpersonal communication. 2. Persuasion
(Rhetoric) 3. Persuasion (Psychology) 4. Influence
(Psychology) 5. Social conflict. 6. Police training.
I. Title. II. Series: American lecture series.
Monograph in American lectures in behavioral science
and law ; no. 1062.
HM132.T48   1983   303.3'4   83-9164

ISBN 978-0-398-04879-2 (hard)   ISBN 978-0-398-06456-3 (paper)

In Memoriam

>*Professor George J. Thompson*
>*Cornell University Law School*

And for

>KELLEY B. THOMPSON
>*and*
>TAYLOR A. THOMPSON

EDITOR'S FOREWORD

THIS book, *Verbal Judo: Words for Street Survival,* by George J. Thompson addresses directly those men and women who engage in one of the toughest jobs imaginable — policing the streets of this country. The book's title, *Verbal Judo,* also refers to all kinds of "confrontation rhetoric," thereby encompassing in its audience any professional who has to deal with the public in a control-management role.

Verbal Judo is both a theoretical and a practical account of how to handle the verbal street encounter. Subtitled "Police Rhetoric," the book offers a rhetorical theory designed specifically for people who have to develop almost instantaneous verbal strategies to control situations non-violently. In order to avoid violence, police officers must change or redirect human behavior with their words. Citizens expect officers to be expert arbiters and negotiators, yet little specific training has been available to develop these important roles. Recognizing that rhetoric is "situational," *Verbal Judo* presents a method and a habit of mind that enables officers to select the best available means of persuasion in any given instant. The book argues that the ability to communicate effectively is an officer's greatest asset, both for his own safety and for the greater good of the community.

Verbal Judo does not suggest that physical force is never necessary. Force is sometimes absolutely necessary and proper, but words are more powerful, correctly used, than often believed. *Verbal Judo's* basic premise is that if officers know the *limits* of words skillfully used, they will know more precisely when force is appropriate.

Verbal Judo argues that rhetorical skill is partially the ability to make oneself into what one has to be in order to handle a situation. It is a practical kind of power. If officers are to be able to create appropriate roles to handle the action they confront, they must know what the communication options are and how these options or strategies can be manipulated and employed functionally.

The book has seven chapters, five of which detail the basic rhetorical elements: perspective, audience, voice, purpose, and organization. Chapters One and Two define the basic problems of street communication and show why the job is so verbally demanding. Because police officers do not "meet" people as others meet people — officers question, interview, and arrest others — their communication problems tend to be more difficult than for other professionals. Thus, the art of communicating with the public *as a police officer* deserves some special and intense study.

Chapter Three, "Perspective," analyzes the way an officer's habitual method of processing reality can hinder or cloud his ability to see clearly. The chapter explores some common biases and assumptions that typically prevent officers from establishing and maintaining an open and flexible mind during a street encounter. It also suggests several techniques officers can use to develop a state of "readiness" for such encounters.

Chapter Four, "Audience," shows how officers can learn to "read" an audience, to see as others see. Because "street savvy" is partly the ability to make oneself into what one has to become to handle a scene, this chapter defines what a rhetorical scene is, how it can be structured, how it may break down, and how it can be controlled using verbal strategies. The chapter also examines different kinds of audiences an officer can expect to confront and offers guidelines for analyzing and responding to them.

Chapter Five, "Voice," discusses how to adopt the proper voice (and tone) for the specific audience. It defines the three basic appeals an officer may use — the rational, the emotional, and the ethical — and describes how to harmonize the voice to the appeal selected. Stressing the chameleon nature of good police work, the chapter illustrates various kinds of voices, roles, and appeals that can be helpful in creating a suitable street "character" to handle difficult situations.

Chapter Six, "Purpose and Organization," defines various kinds of police purposes, shows officers how to define their purpose and handle multiple purposes in one scene, and how to structure their communication to fulfill those purposes. The chapter teaches officers how to use a dramatic sense of structure to achieve their rhetorical ends. The chapter also analyzes how to use legal and departmental guidelines to structure an encounter scene. The author argues that the best structure harmonizes all three approaches to structure: the rhetorical, the legal, and the departmental.

At the end of each chapter are several "mini-cases," which were written to give officers practice in spotting good and bad uses of rhetorical strategies and practice in developing better, more appropriate ways to handle the case problems. Although the cases reflect problems experienced by city police, they are useful for any professional who has to deal with the public in crisis situations, because the principles of *Verbal Judo* can be applied in many different situations.

Verbal Judo, in short, is for the professional who wants to learn how to use others' force and energy to transform potentially explosive encounters into positive resolutions. The bottom line in good police work is officer safety and citizen safety, and the rhetorical skills presented in the text enable officers to approach street encounters with self-confidence in their ability to direct and resolve conflict.

The author, George J. Thompson, is a principal instructor with Communication Strategies, a private communications firm based in Albuquerque, New Mexico. His professional background includes ten years as a university professor as well as five years as a police officer. He has applied his diverse experiences to problems of oral and written communication in widely diverse organizations. He is an expert on situational rhetoric: how language affects people in crisis. He is author of a training manual, also called *Verbal Judo,* which he uses in a program he presents to law-enforcement agencies at various levels. Articles based on his experiences have appeared in the *FBI Enforcement Bulletin* and *The Detective* (the journal of the United States Army Criminal Investigation Division).

Voted an Outstanding Educator of America in 1975, Thompson brings impressive credentials to the writing courses he presents. He directed the composition program at Emporia State University for nine years, and he has developed both remedial and advanced writing courses at the university level. In addition, he has served on projects intended to upgrade writing instruction at the secondary level.

Thompson received his B.A. from Colgate University, his M.A. and Ph.D. degrees from the University of Connecticut, and he completed post-doctoral studies at Princeton University. His diverse personal interests enhance his professional expertise. An avid reader (and reviewer) of detective fiction, he has published numerous articles on Dashiell Hammett. He is also a student of martial arts; he holds a black belt in Judo and a brown belt (with black stripe) in Taekwondo. He feels that his avocation has helped him understand the nature of confrontation and the range of possible responses to threatening situations.

Ralph Slovenko

PREFACE

THIS book is both a theoretical and a practical account of the verbal street encounter, an area that has received very little intensive study. Because of my own experience and interest, I have focused on the police officer, but people in all professions that require changing or modifying human behavior for social good can profit from reading this book. The problem I address — how to use words rather than force to influence people — is of such great social importance that I can only hope that others will join me in trying to improve the training of all personnel who have the thankless task of manning the front lines of defense against social disruption.

The principles and techniques described in this book can be used in practically every verbal encounter, especially in those that involve some degree of conflict, real or potential. To some degree, the many good books on negotiation and conflict resolution have guided my thinking, as have the many books on rhetoric and communication. But few, if any, address the most difficult problem of the immediate street encounter, necessitating, as it does, quick thinking and almost spontaneous verbal response on the part of the officer. I have attempted to tailor my book to this particular arena, an arena in which an officer's rhetorical decisions often make the difference between success and failure, life and death.

As in any new attempt, I am indebted to many, both known and unknown. To the many citizens who endured my own lapses of rhetorical skill as I was learning to be a street officer, I can only give a belated thank you. To the many police officers with whom I worked day in and day out, I owe untold insights about and inspiration for my study of the unique communication situations they experience as a matter of course.

I am indebted to the Emporia Police Department for its continued support and assistance over the last seven years. Chief Ben Janacek and Captain Bruce Fair have greatly assisted my research into training methods on the subject of police rhetoric. The completion of five training tapes on street rhetoric is attributable directly to their cooperation and advice, as are many of the incidents and illustrations used in this book. Indeed, without their support, not a page of this book would have been written. Captain Fair kindly read the text in manuscript and offered countless valued and important suggestions. Though he cannot be held responsible for any weaknesses in this book, he is certainly responsible for any of its strengths.

I wish, also, to thank the English Department and Emporia State University for granting me a sabbatical leave to work full time with the Emporia Police Department and to pursue my research in rhetoric. Moreover, they have been understanding and supportive in what must have been to their eyes a somewhat eccentric field of academic study. To my colleague Denny Clements, who read and re-read my work in progress, I owe an infinite number of stimulating thoughts and suggestions. His encouragement kept me working during the toughest periods, and his diligence prevented numerous stylistic blunders and lapses. To my other colleague, John Somer, I owe a debt of gratitude for his continuing friendship and support during my tenure at Emporia State University. The keen eye of Kate Weigand, my typist, prevented additional blunders in the final manuscript, a fact for which I am most grateful.

My greatest debt is to my family, past and present. To the memory of my grandfather, Professor George J. Thompson of Cornell University Law School, I attribute my abiding belief in the inherent justice and equity of our legal system. It was he who taught me that we must all work to make the law a humanizing force in our society. I can only hope that *Verbal Judo* is one step in that direction. To my grandmother, my surrogate mother, I owe an equal debt: a happy childhood, a fine education, and continued support for my professional work.

To Linda, my wife, who listened patiently and critically to each page of this book and who gave me the necessary emotional support to complete it, I owe an infinite debt. To my daughter, Kelley, and to my son, Taylor, I likewise owe more than I can ever repay. The many nights I was not home because I was on the streets as a police officer — my second job — is but one of their many gifts to me, their daddy. If anything in this book contributes to making this world a better place for them to live, I will feel their sacrifice has been partially rewarded. I can only say that their love and devotion sustained me throughout.

G. J. T.

CONTENTS

VERBAL JUDO

You and your opponent are one.
There is a coexisting relationship between you.
You coexist with your opponent and become his complement,
absorbing his attack and using his force to overcome him.

Bruce Lee

A man who has attained mastery of an art
reveals it in his every action.

Samurai Maxim

To win one hundred victories in
one hundred battles is not the highest skill.
To subdue the enemy without fighting
is the highest skill.
Sun-Tzu

The readiness is all.
Hamlet

INTRODUCTION 1
Problems of Street Communication

*V*ERBAL *Judo: Words for Street Survival* addresses directly those men and women who engage in one of the toughest jobs imaginable — policing the streets of this country. The book's title also refers to all kinds of "confrontation rhetoric," thereby encompassing in its audience any professional who has to deal with the public in a control-management role. Parole officers, social workers, park rangers, social security investigators, psychological case workers, juvenile case workers, even psychiatric nurses and airline security personnel — all have to communicate with others in situations of stress and tension and to maintain control and direction in the encounter scene or they fail. It is to these people that I direct this text, and I hope that something within these pages will help to make their work more efficient, more rewarding, and safe.

Day by day, the job of enforcing the law becomes more difficult. Crime keeps rising, communities expect more and more from their

3

officers, and the legal system, in its entirety, seems bent on frustrating the street officer at every turn. Admittedly, the states and the federal government have tried to help; over the years officers have received better salaries, better equipment, and improved educational opportunities. This has been all to the good, for today officers have a professional standing and a set of expectations that rival those of other respectable professions.

But no amount of money or support can guarantee that the street officer will use good judgment, make the right choices in a situation of stress, or use the most effective words in any given situation. Officers face John Q. Public daily, on a one-to-one basis, and often under trying and emotionally charged circumstances. Whether they will succeed in the one-to-one encounter depends greatly on their individual strengths and weaknesses as human beings. The law serves as one guide for officers, but by itself it is not sufficient to ensure good law enforcement. The legal and departmental codes (local, state, and federal) only tell officers what they *may* do in a situation of particular circumstances, they cannot tell them *how* to do it. This book offers some practical and theoretical advice on the "how" of the street encounter.

Rhetoric is a strange word, possessing several meanings. The oldest and strictest meaning refers to the art of communication. As I use the word throughout the book, rhetoric is *the art of selecting the best available verbal means of communication at any given instant.*

The ability to communicate effectively with the public is, I believe, the most important skill an officer can possess, both for his own safety and for the greater good of the social community. But the task of effective communication is made doubly difficult by the very nature of police work. Police officers do not "meet" people as other ordinary people meet; more often than not, police officers confront some, question others, interview others, and arrest others. Such meetings are unusual communication situations. Even when an officer does not see a meeting with John Q. Public as a "confrontation," the citizen will. Unless, indeed, a citizen is in deep trouble and in need of assistance, any meeting with a police officer will be a disturbing event. Rare is the individual who meets a police officer without feeling anxiety, fear, or anger.

Thus, the communication problem for the officer is more difficult than for other professionals. Police rhetoric, then, or *the art of communication with the public as a police officer,* deserves some special and intense study. Many officers admit that their weakest area of training lies in communication, written or spoken. Generally, police academies offer little in this area other than report writing and some general guidelines for dealing with the public, and few officers arrive at such training centers well versed in the communication arts.

In the more demanding police departments, to be sure, a college education is now required, but even this does not ensure that recruits will have acquired the subtle skills necessary to communicate with precision and effectiveness under stressful circumstances. Courses in classical rhetoric are of little value to the officer-in-training, as are courses in writing and grammar, because they seldom focus on the specific problems posed by the verbal street encounter.

Courses in writing *can* be valuable to officers for their report writing burdens, and indeed much of the latest research that informs modern writing texts can be of some aid to the street officer *if* it is *translated* into concepts and theories that can be *used* by the working cop. *Verbal Judo* aims to provide just such a service; as such, it is a new kind of text, a step into a hitherto dark area of communication theory. In writing this book, I have tried to draw on the best available research in the fields of rhetoric and communication and translate this research into practical street strategies. Many of the strategies we use to teach writing can be applied to strategies for verbal encounters. It is my hope that by reading this text, you, the individual officer, will be able to sharpen your rhetorical skills to the point where you will be able to feel confident in your verbal power under stress. Such confidence makes for professional action on a daily basis.

Verbal Judo does not suggest that physical force is never necessary. Force is sometimes quite necessary and proper, but words are more powerful, when correctly used, than is often believed. To put it another way, if you know the *limits* of words skillfully used, you know more precisely when force is needed. Training in self-defense and the martial arts tells us that force against force is not as effective as learning to move with the force of another. Judo, for example, meaning literally "the gentle way," gives us the power to use another's force to our advantage. So is this true, too, with the skillful use of rhetoric: you size up the person you have contacted and use his energies to achieve your purposes. Police rhetoric, then, is verbal judo, a way to use words and communication strategies to modify or change the behavior of others. Any time an officer manages to defuse another's desire to resist through using the spoken word, he has, in judo terminology, "thrown" him. There can be a far greater sense of self-satisfaction and POWER in talking potentially dangerous subjects into a patrol car than in having to subdue them with the use of physical force.

To perform such feats of rhetorical judo, however, presupposes that the officer will feel confident in his verbal ability, be capable of skillfully reading an audience (the "other"), and be sure of his purpose. This book is designed to help the street officer develop the expertise necessary to use the power of rhetoric in his daily encounters with street people. Being a "street-wise" officer involves mind games and verbal games — strategies intended to keep perpetrators off balance. Some of these "games" are common sense; others require training to work under the pressures of stress and tension. Although many officers possess an innate ability to relate to the people they encounter, some training in theory and practice can improve the chances that they will use such skill more consistently and effectively.

My own personal experience led me to write this text. As a professor of English, whose hobbies have included judo and Taekwondo, I have always been interested in the relationship between words and actions, and the various uses of physical energy. My interest in police work led me into five years of street work, both as a reserve and as a full-time officer. I thus lived in two different worlds: the world of the college professor and the world of the street cop. At first, the most obvious differences struck me. Gradually, however, I came to see that my training in rhetoric and communications could be put to good use in my street work. Having to encounter one stress situation after another, I began to focus on the relationship between language and stress. I found myself playing many different roles during the course of any one shift. Like a stage actor, I learned I had to create my role as I went along. I had to improvise quickly and shift roles effectively, often with little or no warning. I came to see that much of what we call "street savvy" is the ability to create or *make a self* that can harmonize with the street situation.

Rhetorical skill, then, is partially the ability to make yourself what you have to be in order to handle situations. It is clearly more than a "PR" approach to police work, though it can help in this area as well. Primarily, rhetoric is a crucial factor in officer *safety* and *performance*. It is a practical kind of power. If officers are to be able to create appropriate roles to handle the action they confront, they must know what the options of communication are and how these options and strategies can be manipulated and employed functionally.

Verbal Judo explores street communication from this practical angle. The text provides both theory and practice. Each chapter details one of the five basic rhetorical elements: PERSPECTIVE, AUDIENCE, VOICE, PURPOSE, and ORGANIZATION (PAVPO). Each demonstrates how the rhetorical element can be more thoroughly understood and used on the street. At the end of each chapter are several "mini-cases" that are written to give officers practice in spotting good and bad uses of rhetorical strategies and in thinking up better, more appropriate ways to have handled the problem presented. Although the cases generally reflect problems experienced by the city police officer, they can be useful for any professional in control management of human behavior because the principles of shrewd verbal control can be applied in many different situations.

The benefits that can result from good training in rhetorical strategies are numerous, both for administrators and for police officers, which may be reviewed from the following list.

Benefits for Police Administrators:

1. Fewer formal complaints.
2. Fewer informal complaints.
3. Fewer internal affairs investigations.
4. Greater officer efficiency.
5. More efficient retraining of officers who establish a profile of violent street behavior.
6. Better public image for police departments.

Benefits for Officers:

The training will make officers better able to:

1. Control their own biases and PERSPECTIVES.   (P)

2. Analyze an AUDIENCE quickly and skillfully.   (A)
3. Create appropriate VOICES to influence audience. (V)
4. Define and sustain a clear sense of PURPOSE.   (P)
5. ORGANIZE verbal strategies to achieve purpose.   (O)
6. Apply the elements of rhetoric (PAVPO) to the hard realities of the street encounter, i.e. verbal judo.
7. Solve street problems using flexible and alternative thinking.
8. Earn increased respect from the public for professional action.
9. Develop greater self-confidence and self-respect in their work.
10. IMPROVE OFFICER SAFETY — the bottom line in all police work.

Skillful communication can produce such practical and socially beneficial results. Good police work, which involves enforcing the laws of our country in a fair and judicious manner, is a cornerstone of a free society. Ultimately, the benefits that accrue to police administrators and police officers contribute directly to the improvement of society as a whole. It is my hope that *verbal judo* can serve in some small way to strengthen the society we now have.

*To know and to act
are one and the same.*
Samurai Maxim

THE RHETORICAL PERSPECTIVE 2

MORE powerful than mace, the nightstick, or the revolver, effective rhetoric can be an officer's most useful tool in the field. Loosely defined as effective communication, rhetoric is exercised numerous times each day by every officer on duty, whether in civil or criminal matters. Repeatedly, an officer's ability to select the appropriate means of communication, often under surprising and stressful circumstances, is the measure of good police work and good public relations.

Considering the daily pressures of police work — dealing with numerous people whose backgrounds, needs, points of view, and prejudices vary dramatically, moment to moment, as the officer encounters them — it is distressing that so little has been done to prepare officers to anticipate and to handle such complex social situations. Part of an officer's success in handling other people in stress situations comes from a learned habit of mind, a way of viewing the communication situation. The rhetorical perspective is just that — a way of viewing communication, a *stance* one assumes in attempting to deal with others.

The word "rhetoric" is often understood to mean only inflated or exaggerated language, as when one might comment that the president's last speech was "all rhetoric," meaning all froth and no substance. But rhetoric has a second and more classical meaning; from the early Greeks on, it has meant the art or skill of selecting the best available verbal means of persuasion at any given moment. I see it as consisting of five basic elements: perspective, audience, voice, purpose, and organization. The acronym PAVPO represents these five elements.

Perspective may be defined as the viewer's point of view; in the case of an officer on a car stop or at a public disturbance, it is *his* view of the situation. *Audience* is the person (or persons) with whom the officer has made contact. *Voice* is the tone in which the officer conveys his information, his verbal personality. *Purpose* is the officer's goal or end, whether it be an explanation, a warning, or an arrest. *Organization* is the way in which the officer chooses to present or structure his communication; the officer must choose when to say what and how much to say. The shaping of his communication or message often depends on his interpretation of the first four elements of rhetoric and it often determines the eventual outcome of the rhetorical situation.

Perspective, the first P in the acronym PAVPO, is extremely important. The officer's own point of view is generally influenced by the written legal code. On most scenes, an officer represents not himself but society; he is society's spokesman and authority. Yet he is also a human being, with his own personal points of view and biases, and the many typical police calls (e.g. child abuse, beatings, and rapes) wrench his personal feelings, making fair and impartial judgment difficult. As much as possible, the good officer must try to blend his own personal feelings with his sworn legal perspective, letting his humanity come through when it can improve a situation and suppressing it when it threatens to make him an avenger rather than an enforcer of the law.

An officer's task is further complicated by the necessity to understand the perspective of those with whom he is dealing, citizens often quite unlike himself in every way. These citizens, an officer's audience, constitute the most difficult and challenging rhetorical problem for the police officer. Hour by hour during a daily shift, officers carry the pressure of having to see from another's perspective. It is not easy to acquire this habit of mind; it takes practice and training. The ability to achieve a sense of "otherness," a necessary requirement to see from another's point of view, demands a great deal of *disinterest* or non-bias. Sensitive attention to audience, the A in PAVPO, is hard to learn and easy to forget, especially under the day-by-day exigencies of police work.

Consider a typical audience problem, for example. Officers make numerous car stops during an eight-hour shift. After a while, stopping cars becomes just that — stopping *cars*. It is all too easy to forget that one is stopping *people*. Most people have experienced being stopped by an officer; it is rarely a pleasant experience and it is always anxiety producing. Even if no ticket is issued, the driver usually feels inconvenienced and embarrassed. Typically, police officers forget a car stop moments after it has happened, but the person stopped often remembers the event weeks, even months, later and most generally with negative feelings. If an officer has been careless or insensitive in the verbal exchange, it is this that the citizen will remember and nothing else. Too often an officer's reputation, and indeed a whole department's reputation, will be created by the sum of such incidents.

In short, any time a police officer encounters the public, the encounter is apt to have a much more lasting effect on the citizens involved than an officer is likely to anticipate and it will always have at least *a different effect* on the persons involved than it does on the officer; thus the important need for officers to see from the other person's perspective. Admittedly, some officers are born with this ability; others develop it out of a sensitive and compassionate view of their job. The officer who is known to possess "street sense" has this skill — the ability to see disinterestedly — but all officers can develop it by gaining a more thorough knowledge and understanding of the principles of rhetoric. The ability to analyze the precise nature of audience and the ability to act spontaneously on that analysis is one mark of a professional officer. It is often the difference between good and bad police work.

A clear understanding of one's own perspective and that of one's audience aids in the intelligent and judicious selection of tone or *voice,* the V in PAVPO. Most officers know the importance of body language; most know that one's gestures, one's facial expressions, or one's physical stance have the power of one's words. People react to them *as if* they were words. The rhetorical equivalent to body language is voice, the verbal *persona* or character conveyed by one's tone. Every officer knows that if he wants a problem, a resist arrest situation of some sort, it only takes a word or two to get it started. Words can ignite or defuse. The way something is said makes every difference, and tone and diction (word choice) are the determiners. The way in which an officer voices his questions, his commands, or his statements should be a matter of conscious choice. During a typical day, an officer will employ countless different voices in order to create and recreate his public personality again and again. He must be a chameleon, a master of the changeable persona. He becomes the person he must to handle each situation.

Practically every situation calls for a different voice. A car stop one moment, involving an elderly and confused driver, will be followed, perhaps, the next moment by an angry and belligerent driver. An encounter with an erring but respectful teenager, one moment, may well be followed by a sneering and hateful one the next; or literate professionals one moment, the ignorant and illiterate the next. In each case, the officer must respond in a verbal way, but rarely is this "way" the same. When to be polite, even deferential, when to be stern and commanding, when to use the language of the street, and when not — all these problems are rhetorical problems and all demand that the officer know his audience well enough *to create* the best verbal response he can. The voice carries the message; if the voice is wrong or inappropriate, the message, no matter how well-intentioned, will not be accepted without a problem. Indeed, like the professional actor, the police officer must be capable of many voices and many roles, for his audience is never the same. Because so much of his daily work (and its quality) is dependent on the habitual exercise of this skill, an officer should not leave the training of this skill to chance. The study of rhetoric can teach him not only how to understand his own perspective and how to analyze his immediate audience but also how to *choose* and *create* the most appropriate voice to convey his words.

Partly, of course, an officer's choice of voice will be governed by his *purpose,* the second P in the acronym PAVPO. Voice and purpose should be in harmony. Problems arise on the street when an officer's voice is ill-suited to his immediate purpose. If an officer's purpose is to inform, clarify, or persuade, the voice he adopts should be consistent with that purpose. Confusion in any or all of the rhetorical areas of perspective, audience, or voice will lessen an officer's ability to achieve his purpose. In any situation, an officer must have a clear sense of purpose if he hopes to act with consistency and fairness. Unsureness of purpose leads to erratic and confusing behavior — an attribute the officer can ill afford. Matters that call for police attention need an officer to give clarity of direction and purpose, not the reverse. Officers make errors on the street when they confuse intentions, such as the intention to inform with the intention to persuade, or vice versa.

The last element to consider in rhetoric is *organization,* the O in PAVPO. This refers to the problem of structuring a communication or verbal response. There are many ways to structure or shape a single message. An officer in a street scene plays a dual role: he is both actor and primary director. Every street incident is a miniature drama, with its own beginning, middle, and end, but this structure is amenable to countless variations and modifications, most of which are a result of the way in which an officer decides to direct the scene. Police procedure, of course, helps dictate the basic structure; it is the officer's given script. The attempt to determine, for example, whether a driver is under the influence (DWI) has prescribed steps — legal and departmental — that the officer must follow. Beyond this, how the officer will structure the rhetorical encounter with the subject is greatly a matter of improvisation. Like a detective conducting an interrogation, the street officer must decide when to ask what and when to make the actual arrest, if there is to be one. He must direct and shape the encounter. Too much delay may result in a fight; too quick a judgment may have the same end. The officer must not only be professional, he must also *appear* professional, both to the subject involved and to any bystanders in the area. The officer works the public theater of the streets, and much of his professional success depends on how he goes about his job. Should he "muddle" through a car stop or an arrest incident, he can expect problems. The skillful officer knows the procedural and legal script, but he also knows how to structure those steps to fit the particular rhetorical situation.

The acronym PAVPO, then, represents the five elements in every rhetorical situation and officers have to use these elements each day, often unconsciously or spontaneously. The professional learns to manipulate these elements quickly and skillfully; the amateur never learns. Rhetorical expertise is so necessary to good police work that it is surprising that responsible leaders in law enforcement have been generally content to regard it as a pre-employment matter, something a recruit probably has picked up elsewhere. Criminal justice personnel in colleges, universities, and training academies might well consider adding a sixth course to the present five-core curriculum first created by the 1970 Annual California Association of Justice Educators. Such a course, perhaps entitled practical or functional rhetoric, would best be taught by instructors who have police experience and academic credentials. Training academies, particularly, would do well to offer recruits a rigorous course in rhetoric, one that would be specifically designed to meet the realistic demands of the street. Intending to do for the officer what moot court presently does for lawyers, a rhetoric practicum or seminar could, by employing simulation techniques, train officers to make conscious and intelligent rhetorical choices. If approached as a problem-solving course rather than a purely theoretical "book" course, a rhetorical practicum that taught the five elements of rhetoric I have described would significantly improve an officer's street ability and simultaneously enhance his public image — a rare combination.

It is precisely because communication is a dynamic, constantly changing medium that the police officer, perhaps *more* than most professionals, needs to be linguistically flexible and shrewd. At all costs, he must not be deficient in the skills of judgment, tact, and command presence if he is to survive and to be regarded as a true professional. Much of one's judgment, one's tact, and one's command presence is a result of rhetorical skill. Dealing as he does with the public — the hottest possible arena — the police officer must be a master of rhetoric. He must know his own perspective, he must know how to couch his communication, he must be sure of purpose, and he must be clever in the structuring of his message. He must be able to speak in a variety of ways to a variety of people. He is actor and director in countless scenes daily. Ultimately, he should be linguistically rich and rhetorically smooth.

In short, though effective communication may appear spontaneous, it is usually the result of informed instinct and good training, a training that has taught the art of selecting the best verbal mode of response to a given situation. In the past, most officers have had to rely on street experience to give them this training, but such an approach takes time and can be costly and dangerous to everyone concerned when mistakes are made. Officers deserve a better break than this; they deserve as thorough a preparation for the streets as we can give them. The nightstick, the canister of tear gas, and the gun have their place in the street world of the officer, and he generally receives good training with each of them. But because police work is finally more rhetorical than violent, we should prepare each officer to function skillfully and imaginatively, with confidence, in this area.

Control your emotion or
it will control you.
Chinese adage

The angry man will defeat himself
in battle as well as in life.
Samurai maxim

PERSPECTIVE 3
Controlling Point of View

THE POLICE OFFICER AS OBSERVER

PERHAPS the first time an officer realizes the full difficulty of seeing the world clearly is when he has to handle a traffic accident and discovers that among five witnesses, no two can agree on the facts of what happened. So much depends on angle of vision, preoccupation of the observer at the time, and a host of other variables. Few things are as frustrating for an officer as having to piece together, from five different stories, an accurate or probable account of what happened at the time of the accident.

In training academies, officers learn how to question witnesses and how to double and triple check the so-called facts of a scene before they proceed to write the report. They know that citizens do not see well and they accept this as part of the world they live in. Few, however, turn the mirror to themselves and consider how well they see the world. In this chapter, I wish to do just that. I want to consider in some detail the kinds of forces that inhibit accurate assessment of what we, as officers, look at. What influences how we see? How much are we controlled by our hidden and unexamined assumptions about the world? What forces, such as our education or our upbringing, help blur or distort what we look at? How, if at all, can we learn to deal with our own built-in blinders and see more accurately? How, in short, can we draw on our strengths of observation and minimize our weaknesses?

Of the five elements of rhetoric, perspective is the most difficult to analyze, partly because we do not spend much time thinking about who we are or why we think or act the way we do. Think in terms of the following analogy. Each of us wears a specialized pair of glasses, the lenses of which are fashioned from our past experience (including our education) and our gut-level beliefs. When we act (in the street or elsewhere), we *express* our view of the world in some way. When we communicate with others, we *reveal* much about who we are and how we see the world, whether we realize it or not. We all express our hidden assumptions, those beliefs we hold about the *extensional world* (the external world around us) or *intensional world* (our inner world) and the *intensional world* of others (their inner worlds). Any time we make a mistake in our assessment of any one of these worlds, we make mistakes in communication. In many professions, people have the luxury of learning by their mistakes without severe consequence.

It is otherwise with the police officer. Mistakes in communication can endanger an officer's life or those around him, and even the slightest misunderstanding can cause reverberations throughout the community, often producing the "beefs" that sergeants and chiefs have to deal with daily. By job definition, officers on the street represent not themselves but the department and ultimately society. The lenses that each officer looks through are partially formed by the materials of the legal codes, whether local, state, or federal. The legal script colors the lenses an officer wears, but only partially. They are also colored by his past and his immediate present.

PAST EXPERIENCE

An officer's past is both a rich and a treacherous soil. At any moment, what he does in the present may be dictated by what he has experienced in the past. Often these past influences will not be understood or consciously recognized by the officer, but they exist nevertheless. The way in which an officer has been raised, for example, will often influence or even control how he sees a scene in the present. A strict, puritanical upbringing will force a different kind of reaction to a street scene than a more relaxed, more informal one. Thoroughly religious officers will see the world differently than those who are agnostics or atheists. Officers who have experienced child abuse or alcoholism will respond differently than those who have not experienced these things firsthand. Those who are athletic and physical will respond differently than those who are thoughtful and more passive. The list of possible differences is endless, and each recruit to a police academy will have his own particular set of past values, experiences, and expectations.

Training academies try, with what limited time and resources they have, to mold candidates from diverse backgrounds into a unit. But such academies do not have the time, or the duty, to make psychological changes in their officers. They can only hope that the training the recruit receives will produce an officer capable of harmonizing *who* he is with *what* he must become to perform with skill in the field.

What can officers do to help? First, they should analyze their emotional and intellectual makeup, identifying potential danger areas or weaknesses in their personalities. One excellent approach to such analysis is to have the officer examine his personal assumptions about the world, for these gut-level assumptions are one of the greatest potential pitfalls to effective communication and artful negotiation.

Gut-level, emotional beliefs are dangerous because they are based on theories about the world rather than on fact or experiment. Moreover, a further danger lies in treating these assumptions as facts, things obviously so. All people possess such views and they can be positive or negative influences depending on how they are used. Examples of such beliefs are many: God exists; God does not exist;

all men are created equal (or unequal); human life is valuable (or invaluable); people are basically good (or bad); love is everlasting (or fleeting); drunks never reform; longhairs are troublemakers — and so on. The list is endless, and we all live and work with such assumptions.

By their very nature, these beliefs are self-evident. In the world in which the police officer has to deal — a world filled equally with boredom and sudden violence — such assumptions find a rich soil to grow and extend their influence. Because officers often have to make quick, on-the-spot judgments in highly emotional situations, they are pushed into a more black-and-white world than most other citizens; hence, their perspective of the world is likely to be more strikingly influenced by gut-level beliefs or biases, and these weaken their street effectiveness.

In any encounter or situation of negotiation, assumptions play a vital role. To control a situation, an officer must know his own underlying assumptions and anticipate the assumptions of the other. He must be "open" and flexible in point of view, ready to reappraise a situation from moment to moment. From my own experience, I have defined *nine* underlying assumptions that can be potentially dangerous to the officer who holds them as "self-evident." There are, doubtless, countless more, but these nine will illustrate how the gut-level bias can interfere with effective communication.

Assumption 1:	Physical power is an officer's best weapon.
Assumption 2:	Citizens expect officers to use power tactics.
Assumption 3:	Citizens do not like or trust police officers.
Assumption 4:	Fear works more effectively than kindness.
Assumption 5:	Citizens will always resist an officer in some manner.
Assumption 6:	A citizen's attitude or character is expressed by how he dresses and looks.
Assumption 7:	People are basically corrupt.
Assumption 8:	Street people are not open to verbal persuasion.

Assumption 9: Officers distrust words as an effective power tactic.

No one officer will hold all of these nine biases, nor will he necessarily completely believe in one or more of them. But all officers are affected, to some degree, by these or related beliefs. Moreover, in any given situation, any one or more of these assumptions may be true. But none of them is *always* true, and the danger of such views is that these *possibilities* are treated as *probabilities,* and our actions are governed by this perspective.

It is understandable that officers would be susceptible to Assumption 1 that physical power is the most useful kind of power. Our entire culture is saturated with the worship of the physical. Our historical roots — the Revolution and the wild west — have made manhood and violence almost Siamese twins. The police world has always, until very recently, been thoroughly male, and most males have grown up with the attitude that you're not a man if you can't stand "toe-to-toe with some dirt-ball" on the street. Our books, movies, and televisions likewise stress the image of the tough officer, handy with fists, stick, or gun. Many recruits sign up, indeed, precisely because of such dramatic portrayals of police work as *Fort Apache, Police Story,* and *Hill Street Blues.*

But the new officer learns quickly that real police work is not a mirror reflection of the television screen; most of an officer's duties are non-violent, involving him in public relations and innumerable communication situations that cannot be solved by weapons and physical response. Admittedly, weapons training and self-defense are necessary, for when officers need these skills, they need them quickly if they are to survive. But officers who walk the streets ill-equipped with another skill — the strategic use of words — face an equally severe survival problem.

Society increasingly complicates the job for officers inclined to rely on physical power tactics. What officer who has had to draw and fire his weapon can forget the awesome amount of paperwork and investigation that resulted? The law and the community have markedly limited an officer's freedom to use his weapons. One real problem with holding Assumption 1 is that the pistol on the hip is becoming more and more a symbol rather than a useful tool. Such training films as "Shoot, Don't Shoot" reflect society's increased pressure on police departments to train their men to use weapons *only* in absolutely necessary conditions, a guideline difficult to define and even harder to teach.

Men in blue are increasingly watched, evaluated, and even censured when the slightest mishap occurs, and naturally officers are increasingly hesitant in reaching for their weapons. The ability to handle people with words rather than force is more important now than ever, and, therefore, officers should begin to "work out" with words and rhetorical strategies as they would with techniques in self-defense. The first step to such a new orientation is to relinquish Assumption 1; the second step is to learn the art of using words with skill and power.

If officers assume that citizens expect them to react with power persuasion, Assumption 2, they will generally feel obliged to respond to this expectation. The media influence citizens, just as they do police officers, and hence the average guy on the street will regard the officer as a figure of power and physical force. Citizens will often precipitate police violence by expecting or anticipating it. When this occurs, the officer has lost control of the situation, partly because he has been manipulated by the citizen's expectations.

Control and command presence can be established by doing the *unexpected,* reversing expectations. To use words where physical force is expected can unbalance a subject and lead to success for the officer. Where citizens may be inclined to see the role of police officer as a single and narrow one, one defined by a reliance on physical force, officers should see their role as multiple and flexible, open always to adjustment or change given the demands of the immediate situation.

Officers who are rigid in their conception of role definition are subject to manipulation by any intelligent citizen. More than one officer has been "pushed into" overreaction by the promptings of a subject. Street-wise punks know that if they can get officers to overreact, they stand a good chance of escaping whatever the potential consequences might have been. Most citizens, in fact, hope the officer will "blow it" by some form of overreaction so that a letter of complaint can be sent to the chief and a dismissal in court can be expected. Officers should expect, then, that most citizens will encourage, at least to a point, the worst behavior on their part. To many street people, a "roughing up" is well worth the not-guilty verdict; similarly, they know that "being kicked loose" at a scene is often the result of an officer having lost control of the situation so that he dares not report the results. Officers need not be so manipulated; they can be smarter and more flexible in their responses to the would-be agitator.

Assumption 3, that citizens do not like or trust police officers, is equally treacherous, partly because it is true some of the time. John Q. Public wants police on the streets, but he wants other John Q's stopped, not himself. Hence, any time an officer stops a citizen, he is facing a confused ("Why me?") and embarrassed individual at best; at worst, the citizen will also be guilty. To be fair, some citizens will respond to officers in a polite and respectful manner most of the time, but generally most can be expected to voice their inner feelings automatically. The good street officer will generally allow some initial verbal abuse to run its course without comment, tending to the business of getting identification. The weak street officer, one who holds to Assumption 3 rigidly, will take the abuse as evidence that he is disliked as a person and will heighten the level of emotionalism in the scene by directly addressing the initial exasperation of the citizen. The result will be a continuing dialogue that centers on the words of the stopped citizen rather than on the violation for which the citizen was stopped. As pointed out under Assumption 2, such escalation can often derail an otherwise good arrest situation.

True, many citizens do not like or trust the police, but an officer can handle this "truth" when he encounters it in two ways: (1) he can respond personally to it (and this can only derail his legal objectives), or (2) he can expect it to a "reasonable degree" and continue to operate effectively within that reasonable area. No police officer should be expected to put up with undue abuse, but an officer can reasonably expect some initial citizen overreaction and, by anticipating it, *defuse* rather than escalate it. One way to defuse it is to sympathize with it within the stipulated reasonable area mentioned. Another way is to keep foremost in mind that the reaction is not really "personal" at all; the citizen is, in fact, reacting to the city or state or government represented by the officer, not to the officer himself. The symbol of authority is under attack, not the officer, and this perspective helps considerably in maintaining officer equilibrium or poise.

To complicate matters, a citizen who has been stopped will be angry at himself, which may compound an already angry state of mind caused by any number of life's problems. Any time an officer stops and "arrests" someone's daily routine, he is liable to feel the backlash of resentment from the citizen. An officer's best posture during a citizen stop is one of *disinterest,* non-bias, and neutrality, because such a state of mind lessens markedly the chances of overreaction.

To put the matter another way, being "liked" or "disliked" as these terms are normally used should be considered irrelevant. To be liked provides no grounds to overlook a violation any more than to be disliked provides grounds for overreaction. So, too, with the issue of "trust." Within every officer's consciousness lies some resentment concerning public distrust. The individual officer is vulnerable to taunts of police corruption precisely because he is a *symbol* of the profession. Few citizens see officers as individuals; they generally regard officers as types or symbols, and the abuse they heap on the officer represents their view of the profession itself.

To understand citizen overreaction from this perspective can help officers develop a built-in resistance to verbal abuse. To understand the causes for the abuse is to be ready for it; such readiness means the officer will not be blinded by anger or turned from his original purpose. He will not be unbalanced and "thrown" by the abusive citizen.

Assumptions 1 – 3 are equally potential pitfalls to effective communication because if the officer is not careful, he can actually cause negative reactions in his audiences. Like the power of the self-fulfilling prophecy, an officer's basic attitudes can create similar attitudes in his audience, thus stimulating behavior that might have laid dormant or fizzled out had the officer possessed a more neutral perspective. The way one *thinks* governs the way one *acts* and even governs the way others react in response. If an officer enacts Assumptions 1 – 3, he can expect to have difficulty in every encounter.

Assumption 4 states that fear works better than kindness or gentle persuasion in street communication. Partly this is true, but only if the officer is aware of the strategic uses of fear in a controlled situation. Simply to employ fear or intimidation tactics carelessly is ineffective and stupid. Seasoned officers know that no matter how big and bad an officer may be, there is always someone out there who is bigger and badder and it can be any subject at any time.

But consciously and intelligently used, fear can be a useful rhetorical ploy. Consider the typical "good guy, bad guy" strategy that is used by almost every pair of officers at one time or another. One officer threatens and intimidates a subject, usually to excess, and the other officer steps in at an appropriate moment and appears to resist the first officer's tactics by extending kindness and understanding to the subject. Although there are hundreds of variations of this minidrama, each is informed by the same theory: fear sets the stage, but kindness gets the results. The "bad cop" serves as a dramatic foil, a dramatic device to get behind the initial walls of resistance.

In other words, the "good cop" vs. "bad cop" routine is just that — a routine designed to open lines of communication. As such, it is a *rhetorical strategy* that uses fear and kindness alternately. Officers who use it must, like actors, concentrate on timing and control and direct the scene. To accomplish this task, officers must not be blindly attracted to fear as a means. They must, in fact, be open and sensitive to the subject's feelings and changing attitudes if they are to structure the communication drama intelligently. Talking is a *process*, not a product, and as such it is *generative,* meaning that as we talk to a subject our view of him changes as we move through the conversation. Talking, then, is most importantly a process of *making choices,* it is *language in action,* and hence officers must be as open and as non-biased as possible if they wish to make the appropriate verbal and rhetorical choices.

The uses of fear and intimidation do have their place in effective street communication, but they normally cannot stand alone. Kindness, or gentle persuasion, deserves more scrutiny as a strategy. Often kindness will work by itself to produce good results; in other cases, it will work in combination with fear. But officers must come to see that there is nothing "soft" about using kindness to accomplish their purposes. As a device, it opens more lines of communication than it closes because citizens may least expect it from the street officer. Once again, the principle is to unbalance the subject, and kindness can cause an effective reversal of expectations in the officer's favor.

Because talking is a process that requires making choices, even a

single officer can alternate between the extremes of fear and kindness, using first one and then the other in a strategic manner. In
such a case, the officer will play multiple roles, each of which will be
dictated by his subject's response. As long as he is not frozen in one
role, with one overriding assumption, he can maintain the flexibility
to respond shrewdly and skillfully to the rhetorical demands of the
scene. Whether the officer is, in fact, a kind person is irrelevant for
the discussion here; all that is necessary is that he be disinterested
enough to assume the role should it appear effective.

Assumption 5, that citizens always resist an officer, is probably
more wrong than right if by "resistance" we mean real physical, prolonged reaction. The average person in the street is not likely to
want to risk the consequences of such resistance. The citizen knows
the odds are not in his favor. We saw, however, when we examined
Assumptions 1 – 3, that some initial and temporary resistance can
naturally be expected because citizens are distraught and embarrassed when confronted by an officer.

The danger of Assumption 5, then, lies in the expectations that it
raises in the minds of officers as they encounter citizens in the street.
If an officer expects resistance, he will generally read the behavior
patterns of a subject from this perspective and be vulnerable to over-
reacting to the initial burst of resentment that he should expect from
the subject. The officer who holds to Assumption 5 will automatically assume a defensive posture in most encounters; most probably
this defensiveness will trigger increased resistance from the subject.

In a very real sense, whenever we talk with people, we *create* our
own audience: its expectations, its emotional atmosphere, its general
characteristics. Audiences are not *found* things like trees or stones,
they are *made* things, and they are partially made by the speaker. Audiences can shift and change entire natures, depending on the control figure. Police officers come upon an audience and at that
moment it has its defining characteristics; the officer's reaction to
that audience may strengthen those prevailing characteristics or may
change those traits. All will depend on the rapport that the officer attempts to establish. Surely if the officer exudes feelings of defensiveness, his audience will reflect those feelings intensified. If, on the
other hand, he appears to expect cooperation and reflects it in his
command presence, he can move the audience towards that goal. So

much depends on what assumptions the officer brings to the scene, for as soon as he opens his mouth he begins to shape his audience.

Part of an officer's survival skill, his "readiness" for street work, is his ability to gauge the degree and severity of subject resistance. The good officer will have defined for himself a built-in resistance measuring rod that tells him how hot the resistance is and how far it can continue within acceptable limits. Such ability is partly the result of street experience and partly the result of a knowledge of words — their power and influence. Because resistance is not a single phenomenon but an evolving human response to authority, the officer must attempt to be sensitive to its developing rhythms, its rise and fall, its movement.

Moreover, the officer must be sensitive to the immediate situation. What is resistance in one set of circumstances is not in another. As one experienced officer once said to me: "Expect a shove or two when arresting a drunk or DWI and don't make a big deal about it. Resist arrest charges are a lot of paperwork, so reserve them for the real stuff." Each situation has its own unique nature and its own rhetorical potential; officers must fit their actions to the situation if they hope to change or modify it.

That citizens will always resist (Assumption 5) is plainly wrong, and if officers blindly accept it they will be incapable of making the fine discriminations so necessary in defining and distinguishing expected and temporary resistance from sustained and lasting resistance. Just as bad, officers may create sustained resistance where none previously existed. Dangerous resistance is not a *probability* in most citizen-police encounters, though it is always a *possible* one — one that can be made *more* probable by the officer himself if he holds blindly to Assumption 5.

Assumption 6, simply stated as "people are as they appear," can be a tricky one because, as every experienced officer knows, street survival demands that an officer read and interpret his territory at a glance. Clues of dress, appearance, even physical gesture, are important material for the observant officer. It takes a special understanding of an area and the people who populate it to read accurately, and, as more and more police officers drive rather than walk their beats, such familiarity will become increasingly rare.

As young officers pick up street experience, they gradually learn what stereotypes are useful, but such learning can be greatly retarded by the assumptions that they may bring with them from their distant past. Examples are numerous: longhairs are radical, shorthairs are conservative, criminals are more likely to be badly dressed than non-criminals, and so on. The problem is compounded by racial prejudice, which uses a similar technique of equating someone's inner worth with his external characteristics.

The effective street officer learns to shed his deep-rooted prejudices because he knows that these can blind him to the immediate scene. An officer must be a good detective; he must be able to see, to *absorb*, the meaning in the various facial expressions, bodily gestures, or external appearances of his subjects. Every human movement can convey meaning — a tilt of the head, a raised eyebrow, a flush or fidget, a stammer, a sudden hand movement — and the officer must not so pre-judge people that he will misread the clues and subtle hints they unknowingly provide.

Deception is a way of life in the streets; the officer must learn to see through appearances if he is to detect it. He must also learn to use deception in his own way. A chameleon survives by fitting into the landscape, becoming part of the land it works; so, too, must the effective street officer. He must become part of his landscape, constantly shifting roles, and becoming what he must to get the job done. He has to move up and down the social ladder within his community, sifting out information from those who don't want to give it, or locating someone who doesn't want to be found. If he is weighed down by preconceptions and prejudices about people based on physical appearance or racial and ethnic stereotypes, he will be incapable of impartial and effective law enforcement.

Moreover, such an officer is vulnerable to manipulation by others who understand his biased ways of seeing the world. Rigidity in perspective is a weakness; indeed, allowing bias and stereotypical thinking to influence how he approaches and relates to people on the street is as great a weakness as not knowing how to use his nightstick or revolver. In the long run, perhaps it is a greater weakness.

For most police officers, Assumption 7 is clearly true: MAN IS CORRUPT. So much of their perspective is shaped by the "underbelly" of society — the down and out, the angry, the vicious, and the cold-blooded — that it is almost surprising to find an officer who is not tarnished by cynicism or pessimism.

An obvious danger of operating from the assumption that man is corrupt is that officers, particularly the newer recruits, readily adopt the role of avenging angels. The typical scenario of this role is that of the good officer out to punish the evildoers: those who break the law. Breaking the law, thus, becomes a sure sign that a person is corrupt and deserves punishment. The officer becomes judge and jury. The role of peace officer is forgotten in the zeal to root out and eradicate evil in all of its guises. Such officers conveniently forget that they, too, are part of the human race and therefore must, according to the theory, share in the corruption.

Given the job of the police officer, there is some reasonableness to the view that humans are corrupt, but a more realistic assumption would be that human beings are *flawed,* not corrupt. To substitute the word "flawed" for "corrupt" transforms a blinding bias into a useful, more realistic guide to human behavior, particularly street behavior. Officers who hold this modified view will be less susceptible to anger when they confront extremes of human behavior and they will be less likely to pre-judge and pre-sentence those with whom they deal. To understand that human beings have feet of clay, Adam's legacy, is to reserve some compassion for those in trouble or making trouble, and a police officer without compassion is little more than a weapon for an existing power structure.

Further, to operate upon the assumption that people may be flawed rather than corrupt keeps open the possibility that there may be *reasons* for flawed behavior, such as environment, economics, or mental illness. Though no policeman should regard any of these reasons as *excuses* for illegal or anti-social behavior, he might be able to react to such behavior in a more understanding manner and hence be a more effective representative of law and society. To possess and retain an understanding of the social forces that wreak havoc on man daily is to maintain the kind of mental perspective most helpful in allowing him to work skillfully in the area of human relations. Cynicism can defeat an officer's best attempts at communication because it leads him to *believe,* and thus to *act,* as if things could not have been otherwise. The result will be that numerous avenues of persuasion, even of teaching, will be closed to the sight of the officer.

More fitting, perhaps, as a guiding perspective for man collectively is Machiavelli's notion that man is a beast, and if one wishes to control him, he must be a combination of the lion and the fox: the lion for power, the fox for subtlety. Machiavelli was attacking those writers who insisted that man was divine, of god-like potential, and he countered by arguing that man is an animal and hence the animal kingdom provides a suitable analogy for determining how to rule them.

Machiavelli's book, *The Prince,* was written to potential princes and rulers in the sixteenth century, but his advice offers some interesting guidelines for street officers in the twentieth century. Man is neither good nor evil; he is, rather, an animal that can be effectively controlled by combining force and intelligence. Though many humanists would probably object to this perspective of man, for police officers who have to deal with the worst of human nature on a daily basis, this Machiavellian point of view is most helpful. For one, it does not lead to cynicism as easily as the more optimistic views of man are liable to because the officer is not constantly being disappointed by the human behavior that he does confront. Moreover, the Machiavellian perspective is not negative, it is neutral and descriptive. One of the essential necessities for every officer in street encounters is *control;* he must maintain control at all costs. If he can employ force and intelligence at the correct moments (alternate power with subtlety), he has a good chance of doing his job well.

To assume that man is corrupt, Assumption 7, is to adopt a perspective that narrows the possible options to communication; to assume that man is flawed rather than evil is to hold a view that can open lines of communication. Officers who train their minds to regard human beings as controllable through the alternative uses of force and intelligence — the Machiavellian perspective — are better able to understand the principles of rhetorical strategies.

Assumptions 8 and 9 work together to weaken further an officer's tendency to relate to people verbally. Assumption 8 states that street people are incapable of responding to verbal persuasion. Generally, officers will reserve this point of view for those habitual troublemakers that they encounter during a typical shift. This belief is strengthened by an underlying belief that most people who break the law are stupid and hence only capable of understanding force (see Assumptions 1 and 4). Moreover, officers who deal with the same street people repeatedly tend to develop a *habitual mode of response* to them. When this occurs, little improvement can be expected in the relationships, and officers will lose the opportunities to change the nature of their rhetorical stances towards the subjects.

The development of the "frozen rhetorical stance" is best seen in police encounters with the habitual offender, particularly the juvenile. Officers can have real trouble relating to the youthful offender, partly because of the assumption that teenagers don't listen anyway, and partly because of the gut-level assumption that kids should respect their elders. Such beliefs do not facilitate street work, they only hinder it. Officers need to develop a sense of "otherness," a sense of what it might be like to see through the eyes of their subjects and then construct verbal means to relate to those subjects.

Such "otherness" can only be developed if officers assume that their subjects are capable of understanding, at least at some level; the skillful officers will attempt to find these levels and open communication lines using whatever verbal means they can discover. Such "discovery" may take numerous verbal probes. To be rebuffed several times does not prove that a subject is unreachable, it may only mean that the right approach has not been found.

In the chapter on "Audience," we will explore several ways to analyze and communicate with a subject. For now the emphasis is on how the perspective of officers can close down lines of communication even before they have a chance to open. To believe that street people, particularly the habitual offender or the juvenile, cannot be reached with words destroys any rhetorical power that officers might possess. A closed mind results in a rigid rhetorical stance, a dangerous liability for any officer.

Assumption 9, the converse of 8, inhibits officers from attempting verbal persuasion as often as they might because they feel verbally *inferior* to many of the citizens they encounter each day. Police work has never been thought of as being a "verbal profession," strangely, and hence it is not surprising to find among those who enter the profession a profound *distrust* of words, even of higher education itself.

Although such distrust may be gradually disappearing, it still prevails. English and communication courses are typically regarded as "bullshit" courses, impractical courses, and the word "rhetoric," if it is understood at all, is taken to mean exaggerated and inflated talk. Officers tend, therefore, to think in terms of physical action rather than verbal action — a tendency which blinds them to rhetorical strategy. Ironically, though officers may feel that communication skills are so much "BS," they grudgingly realize that the professionals in their communities possess these skills and wield them powerfully. Being untrained in their use or feeling inadequate in their exercise, officers fall back on reticence and physical action.

Where Assumption 8 seemed to rest on an attitude of superiority (that is, the subject is too stupid to respond to words), Assumption 9 rests on an inferiority complex (i.e. "Verbal skill is not my strength"), and together both assumptions increase distrust and resistance to the arts of verbal strategy. Because police work is so heavily rhetorical and so dependent on skillful verbal control and response, officers must learn to use whatever verbal superiority they may have over the street person and increase their own skills in the communication arts to deal with the professional. By doing so, officers can lessen the negative effects of both Assumptions 8 and 9.

In short, officers must review their pasts, examine their most cherished assumptions, and learn to integrate *who they have been* with *who they must become* if they wish to be effective in the streets. The nine assumptions that we have analyzed are present in many of us — officers and citizens — but these nine, and others like them, must not rule our conduct in the present. Rigidity is weakness, flexibility is strength. Effective officers are those who know how to read present situations accurately and who can respond to them in flexible and controlled ways.

THE PRESENT: ITS CONSTRAINTS

Learning to let the present situation dictate proper street response is one means of establishing a proper perspective. Every street encounter has its atmosphere and its potential drama. Every scene has its own rhetorical constraints and its obstacles. The officers on the scene, the subject or subjects (i.e. the audience), bystanders, the hour of the call, the particular environment, even the weather — all of these are potential obstacles to effective communication. Because such obstacles can have a marked influence on how an officer will *see* a scene, they influence how he will respond to it.

Consider what forces act on an officer in a typical street encounter with a disorderly subject. The officer's view of the scene will be partly influenced by his present state of mind. He may be angry and frustrated over a previous call, or he may be bored and tired, or he may be relaxed and cheerful — any combination of such feelings is possible. Moreover, should he have a partner, his mood may be influenced by their relationship at the moment. Further, the location of the call, the time of day or night, the weather, even the nature of the call itself, all have an effect on the officer as he arrives. Carrying these pressures, the officer must approach and deal with the disorderly subject that is the occasion for the call. The loud and abusive language of the subject is another constraint in the rhetorical scene.

Few citizens ever have to communicate in situations this fraught with tension and stress and few would be able to handle it well, but the officer must. He not only has to be on the scene, he is expected to bring control and equitable decision making to it. He must be *ready* to handle his own possible inner turmoil while simultaneously handling the street turmoil.

To accomplish such a difficult communication task, the officer must be capable of reading the scene, the clues put forth by the rhetorical constraints mentioned. Any one or more of the nine assumptions we analyzed can hinder this reading, as can any biased reaction to present constraints. The officer's best approach will be an assumed *disinterest,* a state of mind ready to be as flexible and as open as possible; in such a mental state, the officer will be able to sift the available clues and to pattern them in an efficient manner to handle the problem. The greater the disinterest, the greater the chance of seeing literally and imaginatively, and hence the greater the possibility of fashioning a proper verbal and rhetorical approach strategy.

The concept of "disinterest" is one that all officers should come to understand and appreciate, for it can improve their communication skills twice over and make them "ready" for the changing scenes that they will face daily. Disinterest means free from bias, impartial; it does not mean UNinterested or mechanical. It does not mean unconcerned with the citizen's problems. The state of disinterest is marked by qualities of open-mindedness and flexibility of judgment.

It is *seeing* before *judging*. Its opposite is bias, prejudice, and self-interest.

Indeed, all successful actors, martial artists, and athletes in general know the value of disinterest. A good stage actor puts his all into becoming the role assigned. People who can't act are those who are overly self-conscious and too aware of themselves to adopt a role with any realism. Someone trained in self-defense responds automatically to the demands of the immediate threatening situation. He subsumes his "self" into the energies of his antagonist and reacts from a kind of "still center." All good athletes know the inner feeling of selflessness experienced in moments of great tension or stress; without it, they would be unable to perform. They would "freeze" and fail to do what had to be done. Such might be the tennis player who beats all his teammates in practice but who always loses in the varsity matches because "he can't get into his rhythm." Too aware of himself on the spot, he lets his ego get in the way of performance and he fails.

The street officer, like the actor or athlete, must learn to subsume his ego and sense of "self" into the multiple roles that he must play. Like the actor, the officer has a "script," the law, but it is incomplete as a guide to action. The officer must complete the role he finds himself playing in each street encounter. He must *improvise* given the peculiarities of the street scene. If he wishes to control a scene, he must communicate effectively with the subjects concerned and he must not allow his ego to hinder his management of people.

Biases and prejudices, like too much self-conscious ego, prevent officers from responding effectively to the ever-changing street scene. Rigidity in perspective is the result of being controlled by one's past assumptions and/or by one's present ruling biases. Officers who wish to control communication situations must first learn to control themselves, inwardly and outwardly, and this process begins with the awareness of SELF.

The second part of the learning process involves understanding several techniques that can improve street analysis and guide an officer's street response. Each technique, if followed closely, will minimize *personal* reaction and maximize professional response by stressing the use of the "disinterested perspective."

SPECIFIC TECHNIQUES TO SEE DISINTERESTEDLY

Any technique that facilitates observation must be bias-free and useable in a variety of different situations. Moreover, it should be flexible and sensitive to the rhetorical situation and be "generative" in the sense that its procedures lead officers through a range of processes that trigger insight and give shape to chaos. Such procedures are called "heuristics" because they are defined ways to solve problems. The value of a heuristic lies in its power to guide an observer through a problem in a disinterested manner. Such an approach diminishes the power of the biases and assumptions we examined earlier and aids officers in controlling the power of the present constraints in any given scene. Because a heuristic strengthens a person's ability to see and pattern details, it can help an officer *act* on the meaning of those details and patterns in each particular encounter scene.

Technique 1: The 5 W's and 1 H Heuristic

Journalists, for whom this technique is a favorite, have learned to ask the six crucial questions in any scene: Who? What? Where? When? Why? How? Like police, journalists have to be ready to gather facts, data, opinion, even conflicting pieces of information, and make some sense out of a situation whether it be a traffic accident, a shooting, or a political convention. Once they have understood a scene as well as they can, they leave to write up their articles; they have the luxury of having only to be in attendance; they do not, like the officer, have to deal actively with the scene itself. A journalist's communication problems come later, over a typewriter; an officer's problems come immediately, while in the midst of the scene. He has to discover the answers to the six questions and then act on this information. Not to know the answers to these six basic questions can lead to poor communication and to bad arrests.

Arriving on a scene, an officer must efficiently discover WHAT happened, WHO the principals are, the WHERE and the WHEN of the incident, and the WHY and the HOW, if possible. Any one or more of these six elements can be unclear or problematic; any one or more can be other than it appears. Foremost in the officer's mind must be his safety and his quest for the answers to these six questions. Not to know can get an officer killed. The WHO and the WHAT are crucial in any scene, for without a clear knowledge of these two, an officer cannot apply the legal code. Often, indeed, the WHO will be in dispute among present parties: WHO punched WHOM first? WHOSE bottle or WHOSE bag of grass is it? WHO was actually on the scene when the event happened? And so on. Moreover, the WHAT will often be unclear: WHAT actually transpired? WHAT were the precise sequences of action that took place? WHAT violation of the law is at issue?

To address these six questions first, rather than one's own preoccupation or emotional state, is the beginning of good law enforcement. Effective street officers allow these questions to guide their behavior in dealing with street problems; accuracy of observation and perception are central; they delay judgments as long as possible. In trying to communicate effectively with the parties involved and to discover the best solutions to the street problem in front of them, skillful officers attempt to be sensitive to the shifting priority of the six questions, given the particular situation that they face. In terms of officer safety, the WHO and the WHAT are almost always primary, but the WHEN, WHERE, WHY, and HOW can and do vary in importance from scene to scene. In one instance, the WHERE and the WHY may be crucial, in another, irrelevant.

Generally, the WHY and the HOW will be important for the officer to decide what law or ordinance to use; indeed, the WHY is often crucial in the officer's attempt to decide what verbal strategy would best fit the situation. Deciding about the *causes* of a street problem can usually help an officer fashion a verbal approach that will communicate and influence a subject who might otherwise be unreachable. To look for causes before acting may prevent, for example, an officer mistaking an accidental act for an intentional one or vice versa. Moreover, to show a subject that the causes of his actions are understood, even if not condoned, often lessens the initial hostility that the subject may feel for the officer and improve, thereby, the officer's chances of influencing the subject through words rather than through force.

In other words, one method of avoiding the needless verbal confrontations that can arise from citizen overreaction (that is, that "reasonable degree of expressed frustration") is for the officer to employ the 5 W's and 1 H heuristic. This heuristic or procedure helps an officer maintain a "professional cool" in the midst of a heated present. Unless an officer finds himself facing an extreme situation (for example, a violent in-progress incident) he should take no physical action or make any firm judgments until the six relevant questions have been explored. Lack of knowledge can lead an officer into blundering, overreaction, and bad arrests. The 5 W's and 1 H is a basic thinking tool that officers can use to discover what they know and what they don't know, to see a pattern in a seemingly chaotic series of events, and to select an appropriate means of response.

Technique 2: The Four Criteria for Determining Means and Ends

Most street problems involve officers in making decisions about *means* and *ends*. Officers continually have to take positions regarding street incidents because they have to *arbitrate* between extreme positions. Scenes that call for police action are generally "hot" situations, events calling for third-party intervention. Such "crisis intervention" is always a matter of problem solving for the officer, and problem solving is a skill that often requires a systematic, step-by-step approach. The 5 W's and 1 H heuristic is a necessary tool in such situations, but it is not sufficient. That is, in many cases, facts alone will not tell an officer what must be done. They may indicate what laws are involved, but they cannot tell an officer *how* he should handle a problem or even how he ought to *evaluate* the various options open to him should there by any. *Means* are usually problematic: that is, in any situation there may be several possible approaches to bringing it to a successful close, and the officer's decision will be the result of his evaluation of these options.

Officers can successfully employ the following *Four Criteria* to discover the best rhetorical strategy to handle the specific situation they face. The functional question throughout any scene is always, "What is the best tack to take in this instance given these particular constraints and problems?" In considering alternatives and options, officers can ask the following four questions:

  1. Is this option PRACTICAL? That is, given the situation, is

this option or alternative possible?

2. Is this option EFFICIENT? That is, is it economical, manageable? Will it produce the effect with a minimum of waste and effort?

3. Is the option WORKABLE? That is, will this mean or set of means actually produce the desired *effect?* Will it produce what I want it to?

4. Is the option CONSISTENT WITH OTHER VALUES? That is, will the means square with the expressed values of the end? Is the option consistent with present legal, ethical, or social values?

Each of these four questions or criteria demands that the officer view the question of *means* from a slightly different perspective. All four together provide a complete reading of the range of possibilities open to the officer at the moment, thus helping to guide his choice of rhetorical strategy. Moreover, like the 5 W's and 1 H procedure, the Four Criteria help officers develop and maintain *disinterest* because they concentrate officers' attention on the immediate situation rather than on their own emotions or biases. As a set of procedures (that is, a heuristic), the Four Criteria can serve as an excellent guide to effective decision making.

How can officers use these questions in the field? First, they must be aware that in any given scene, the relative importance of the questions will vary. In one instance, EFFICIENCY might be the crucial question, the others subordinate; in a second scene, PRACTICALITY might be dominant. Although in every scene an officer should ask all four questions, he will order the priority of the questions differently in each new instance.

Consider a street encounter in which an intoxicated subject is causing a disturbance and the officer arrives to find that the subject has several friends with him who are amused by his drunken behavior. Others on the street, however, are not amused and a confrontation appears likely. Suppose, also, that the officer does not have a backlog of calls and so he is not rushed. What to do? How can the situation best be handled? In considering question one (i.e. What is PRACTICAL or feasible), the officer must determine what he has to work with in this particular scene: he is alone, there are several subjects supporting the disorderly subject, and there are just as many desiring to shut the subject up. There is also the subject himself, and the officer must decide how much influence he can have over the subject using only words. If the subject is too intoxicated to listen or respond to words, then a quick and efficient arrest is the only alternative. The officer will have to expend his rhetorical energies convincing the subject's friends that he is better off in jail for the night and calming the anger of the hostile bystanders.

On the other hand, should the subject be capable of understanding the English language, the officer can analyze his options using the Four Criteria. Although talking to the subject for a prolonged period might seem INEFFICIENT in terms of time, it might be a PRACTICAL and WORKABLE approach to the problem if the officer can convince the subject that staying off the streets for the night is preferable to spending a night in jail. The approach will be WORKABLE or efficacious if it produces the desired result, which is getting the subject off the streets. As an option, this approach would rank high in the VALUE area as well, for if it succeeds, the officer will save time and paperwork as well as prevent potential violence.

In this scene, then, talking the subject into leaving the scene appears to be the most PRACTICAL and WORKABLE approach and is clearly consistent with other values, such as citizen and officer safety. In a different case, taking the time to talk might be dangerous for the officer or others and hence would be IMPRACTICAL, UN-WORKABLE, and contrary to VALUES. Generally, in scenes in which an officer decides that time and safety are of the essence, the best rhetorical response is one of the "unalterable decision." When there is only one decision that can be made given particular circumstances, the officer should word this message clearly and forcefully. Command presence is partially the result of absolute clarity; the subject must know that there exists but one choice: "Get into the car, now. You are under arrest." An officer can create problems by not communicating to a subject that his decision is "unalterable." Any ambiguity or vagueness suggests to the subject that there may be other options and often he will act out this belief either by arguing with the officer or by physically resisting him.

When we analyze PURPOSE, we will see again how the Four

Criteria can be used. For now, the point is that whenever an officer encounters a citizen in a confrontation situation, he has at least three sets of procedures that he can use to guide his response, each of which helps to ensure that he will not react solely on the basis of his gut-level assumptions or according to his emotional state. The first is, of course, the written code, the law, with any accompanying departmental regulations and guidelines. The second is the 5 W's and 1 H procedure that helps the officer gather important data. The third is the Four Criteria procedure that can measurably improve an officer's ability to consider options and select the most appropriate for the particular instance. Informing all three procedures should be a sensitive awareness to the pitfalls of the personal perspective and an acceptance of the fact that when an individual puts on a uniform, he becomes more than himself; he becomes a representative and symbol of his community and society and he should conduct himself in this spirit.

MINI-CASES ON PERSPECTIVE

General Directions

1. Read each case through twice to become familiar with all the details.
2. Note, particularly, the situation and the officers' attitudes and perspectives regarding it. How do these influence, for good or bad, what happens in the scene?
3. Using the materials in this chapter, list the effective rhetorical decisions in each case and provide reasons for their effectiveness. Do the same for the poor decisions that you spot.
4. Be prepared to suggest better or more appropriate ways to have handled the problem.

Case 1: "The Smith Case" (Version 1)

At 0100 hours Officer Smith receives a call to respond to a disorderly subject in the alleyway of the 500 block of Commercial Street behind the Bear Claw Tavern.

Two minutes later Officer Smith pulls into the alley and sees a large white male, approximately 6′5″ tall, 245 pounds, shaking his fist at a group of bystanders, one of whom Officer Smith recognizes as the tavern owner. As he leaves his vehicle, Smith requests a second officer to respond to the call.

As Officer Smith walks towards the subject, the subject turns and shouts, "Hey, you mother, leave me alone before you get hurt. No fucking barkeep is gonna tell me to leave his place!"

The tavern owner walks over and tells Officer Smith he wants to file a complaint against the subject for disorderly conduct. He claims the subject smashed a table, broke several glasses, and chased several patrons from his tavern.

Just then the second officer drives up and Officer Smith tells him to go into the Bear Claw Tavern and check out the damages and interview anyone who had seen the event take place. The second officer enters the tavern with two or three witnesses.

As the angry subject walks up to Officer Smith, Smith says,

"Calm down, man. Calm down. What's your side of this?"

"Ain't no side to it, Jack. Them in there started it and I finished it. That's all. You ain't taking me in for shit."

"I'm gonna have to if the other officer can verify the owner's story. The owner wants to sign a complaint against you. Let's see some ID, please."

"I ain't showing you shit, Jack. I may have been drinking, but I'm right, and you ain't big enough to take me by yourself."

"I'm sure you're right. You're twice as big and you look tough enough, that's for sure. But can you afford to take the rap for assault and battery and resist, against a police officer? Right now, if you're guilty, we're talking $25 to $50 fine; you swing on me and you'll be looking at a $500 fine and possibly some jail time. You got that much money or time? Why play it hard when it can go so easy?"

The second officer reappears and nods to Officer Smith, saying, "We got to go with him. The owner's story checks out."

"Now we don't have any choice, man," says Smith to the subject. "You got to go, one way or the other. Easy and cheap one way; hard and expensive the other. Which do you want? It's nothing personal; we just don't have a choice."

The subject takes his wallet out, throws it on top of the patrol car, and turns around. "I ain't got that kind of money, Jack. Let's go it easy."

ANALYSIS: From the clues given, *describe* as thoroughly as you can the subject's point of view at the time the officer enters the scene.

ANALYSIS: From your reading on Officer Perspective, what *strengths* did Officer Smith show in dealing with the subject? What considerations seemed to guide his handling of the scene? What pitfalls, from a rhetorical point of view, did he avoid? (Think of the Four Criteria in evaluating the scene.) Do you spot any *weaknesses?*

Case 1: "The Smith Case" (Version 2)

At 0100 hours Officer Smith receives a call to respond to a disorderly subject in the alleyway of the 500 block of Commercial Street behind the Bear Claw Tavern.

Two minutes later Officer Smith pulls into the alley and sees a large white male, approximately 6'5" tall, 245 pounds, shaking his fists at a group of bystanders, one of whom Officer Smith recognizes as the tavern owner. As he leaves his vehicle, Smith requests a second officer to respond to the scene.

As Officer Smith walks towards the subject, the subject turns and shouts, "Hey, you mother, leave me alone before you get hurt. No fucking barkeep is gonna tell me to leave his place!"

The tavern owner walks over and tells Officer Smith he wants to file a complaint against the subject for disorderly conduct. He claims the subject smashed a table, broke several glasses, and chased several patrons from his tavern.

Just then the second officer drives up and Officer Smith tells him to go into the tavern and check out the damages and to interview anyone who had seen the event take place. The second officer enters the tavern and two or three witnesses are with him.

As the angry subject walks up to Officer Smith, Smith says, "Let's not have any more mouth. Break out your license or some ID."

"I'll be as mouthy as I want goddamn it! I don't have to take any crap off you. Them in there started it and I finished it, that's all. You ain't gonna hassle me."

"I'll hassle you all I want if the other officer verifies what the tavern owner said you did in there. Now hand me your ID and be quick about it."

"I ain't showing you shit, Jack. I may have had a few beers but I'm right, and you ain't tough enough to take me, anyways."

At this moment the subject's girl friend runs up to him and grabs his arm, saying, "Come on, Mike. Let's get out of here. You know cops love to give people trouble. Let's go."

"He's not going anywhere, honey. Your man here is talking himself into a pair of cuffs, aren't you, buddy?" says Officer Smith.

"Yeah? Who says? You? Big bad cop, huh? Why don't you try to take my ID, Jack, if you're so tough. I'll put you down, man, down right here in the alley, right where you belong."

The gathering crowd of bystanders begin to yell encouragement to the subject and to berate Officer Smith. ("Yeah, give it to him, Mike, pound him!"; "Hey, chicken little with the badge, whatcha gonna do now?" etc.)

Officer Smith reaches for the subject's shoulder. "Come on, asshole, in the car; you're under arrest for resist."

The subject spins away from Officer Smith's grasp and throws a right hand to the face, catching Smith a glancing blow on the forehead, knocking his hat off. Smith and the subject wrestle around, and Smith manages to bend the subject over the fender of his patrol car. The subject is kicking and shouting, "Lemme go, motherfucker!" The subject's girl friend tries to grab one of Officer Smith's arms, and several other bystanders approach as if to get into it also.

Just then the second officer comes out of the tavern and he quickly disperses the crowd and frees Officer Smith from the clutches of the screaming and kicking girl friend. "Come on, everyone, beat it; that's enough for one night. This man is going to jail."

Between the two of them, the officers get the subject cuffed and put into the patrol car. The second officer says to Smith, "Well, the tavern owner's story checks with those inside. We got enough to go with disorderly, destruction of private property, and resist arrest. What the hell happened here while I was inside?"

"The guy got what he asked for, that's what!" said Smith.

ANALYSIS: From the clues given, *describe* as thoroughly as you can the subject's point of view at the time the officer enters the scene.

ANALYSIS: From your reading on Officer Perspective, what *weaknesses* did Officer Smith exhibit in dealing with the subject? What assumptions seem to guide his verbal response to the subject? What criteria for action does he ignore? (See the Four Criteria, p. 36.)

Case 3: "The Officer Behr Episode"

Officer Behr has forty minutes left in his evening shift. He has had a bad day: one resist situation and three car stops in the last hour, in each of which Officer Behr had taken more than his share of verbal abuse. He is tired and angry at the world, and he is running radar at 49th and Chestnut, where the speed limit is 20 mph.

Officer Behr wants one more ticket, one more "pinkie" to hand the next abusive citizen. His hand-held radar picks up a vehicle moving 33 in the 20 — just right for a tickie. He stops the car three blocks away. As he approaches it, a young man sticks his head out the window and says, "What's your problem, officer? I haven't done nothing!"

"It's not my problem, Jack, but yours! Let's see your license."

The driver springs out of the car, saying, "Who you calling Jack, anyway? You got no call to stop and insult me! You cops are all the same, always looking to pick on someone, ain't you?"

"Shut up, get back in the car, and break your license loose, NOW!"

"Fuck you! I don't have to get back in. I'll just stand here, and there ain't nothing you can do about it! Here's my license!" (Subject throws license on top of the car.) "Whatcha stop me for, anyway, just to hassle me?"

"I clocked you 33 in a 20, bud, that's why, and you're getting a tickie. How do you like that, mouth?"

DIRECTIONS: Using the Four Criteria to determine means and ends, analyze Officer Behr's actions. Particularly, which criterion does he fail to consider? What are the consequences? What PRESENT CONSTRAINTS influence Officer Behr's perspective? What PAST CONSTRAINTS influence his perspective? What other WEAKNESSES in his citizen contact do you notice? Any STRENGTHS?

In order to achieve victory
you must place yourself in your opponent's skin.
If you don't understand yourself,
you will lose one hundred percent of the time.
If you understand yourself,
you will win fifty percent of the time.
If you understand yourself and your opponent
you will win one hundred percent of the time.
Tsutomu Oshima

AUDIENCE 4
The Art of Knowing the Other

IN the last chapter we looked at the problems of controlling personal point of view, our PERSPECTIVE. In this chapter we switch the focus to the other guy, the AUDIENCE. The ability to *read* an audience is a crucial skill for patrol officers; it is the key to officer safety, the bottom line in police work.

One truth an officer must never forget is that *scenes change with his entrance into them.* Scenes have their own dynamics, their own rhythm, long before an officer arrives. Everyone has had the experience of watching children at play or friends at a party and, wanting to capture the moment on film, attempted to enter the scene, camera in hand. At this moment of entrance, things *change*. People become self-conscious, poses tend to replace spontaneous behavior, and getting "good shots" becomes a very difficult task. Whatever is taken is different than it would have been had a hidden camera been employed.

The fact is, *events change because of certain kinds of presences.* When you, as officer, enter a scene, you cause an alteration of the scene by your very presence. It is important that you think in terms of two worlds: the world *before* you entered it (the scene as it is being played out) and the world as it becomes given your presence. People act differently under different circumstances, and your entrance creates a *new* set of circumstances.

Audience sensitivity is achieved only if you can see through the eyes of others; that is, see the scene as it must have been before you entered. To do this, you must dislodge yourself from your own self-referential world and from the biases and assumptions that you bring with you into the scene. Street awareness is really the mental process of *seeing into* the full psychological dynamics of the situation that you face; if you can do this, you will be able to *anticipate* events and actions before they take place. Such anticipation allows you to make the necessary adjustments in your physical and verbal approach to a scene.

To see into a scene, or to see through the eyes of others, involves some degree of *disinterest,* some degree of *common sense,* and some degree of *rhetorical sensitivity.* Above all, it requires a sure sense of the total *rhetorical situation* at hand.

THE RHETORICAL SITUATION

Lloyd Bitzer, an academic rhetorician, has argued that "a rhetorical situation is a natural context of persons, events, objects, relations, and an exigence which strongly invites utterance. . . ."* By "exigence," he means a problem or an obstacle to overcome. He goes on to say that rhetoric is always *situational;* that is, rhetoric comes "into existence as a response to a situation, in the same sense that an answer comes into existence in response to a question, or a solution in response to a problem" (Bitzer, 1971, pp. 385 – 386). He sees

---

*Bitzer, Lloyd: The rhetorical situation. In Johannesen, Richard L. (Ed.): *Contemporary Theories of Rhetoric: Selected Readings* (New York: Harper & Row, 1971), p. 385. Further citations in text.

rhetoric as a mode of altering reality through talk, which changes the behavior of the audience involved.

Professor Bitzer's analysis of the rhetorical situation is helpful for our purposes because he specifies four parts that make up the rhetorical situation.

1. The first is an actual or a potential EXIGENCE or problem in the situation that can be modified or changed through verbal persuasion. The problem is an imperfection or obstacle and is marked by urgency. According to Bitzer, it is "something waiting to be done, a thing which is other than it should be" (1971, p. 386). Not all problems are rhetorical. Things that cannot be changed by talk (e.g. floods, storms, natural disasters, or a man pulling and firing a pistol at you) are not rhetorical. Events that call for physical action or self-defense have passed the rhetorical stage and call for a non-verbal response.

Bitzer makes the additional point that in any situation, *one* problem will be the controlling force, the shaping principle of the scene, and as such it will specify the audience to be addressed and the change to be effected (1971, p. 387). Such problems or exigencies can be real or unreal depending on how they are perceived — important or trivial, simple or complex. To communicate with an audience, you have to attempt to see the world as others see it; you have to be able to *read* the perspectives of those with whom you deal. For example, a man who wants to kill his child because he believes it issued from the devil presents you, as police officer, with a very real *unreal* exigency. You know he is "crazy," but if you are to get through to him and modify or change his behavior, you will have to begin with his perspective, not your own. In this illustration, the *problem* is his potential action (killing his child) and it will serve as the organizing principle of the scene, particularly if the subject has a knife at the throat of his child.

2. The second element of the rhetorical situation is the AUDIENCE. This audience must be capable of being influenced by words. Types of audiences can range from a single person, known or unknown, to a group, known or unknown, to multiple groups, known or unknown. The type of audience, and how much you know about it, will partially determine your rhetorical success.

3. The third element in the rhetorical situation is what Bitzer

calls the "SET OF CONSTRAINTS" in the given situation. Constraints are such things as other persons, events, objects, and relations that are part of the situation "because they have the power to constrain decision and action needed to modify the exigence" (Bitzer, 1971, p. 385). Such things as beliefs, attitudes, facts, motives, interests, time of day or night, and weather are all examples of typical constraints. In the case of the man with the knife at his child's throat, one crucial constraint is his *belief* that his children have been infected with the devil. Other constraints might be the distance that he is from the nearest officer and his state of present agitation. An officer stepping into this scene will have to attempt to create discourse that will address the *exigency* at hand, the particular *audience* involved, and the precise *set of constraints* present in the situation.

4. The fourth and final element is, of course, the OFFICER HIMSELF, complete with his arguments, personality, and style of handling the scene. His discourse or verbal persuasion is the last and key ingredient. His difficult task is to evaluate correctly the crucial *exigency,* read his particular *audience,* respond to the inescapable *constraints,* and to find the right words to modify or change the existing state of affairs.

Types of Rhetorical Situations

A rhetorical situation, therefore, is made up of *four* major components: the *audience,* the *problem* or defect that requires change (the exigency), the set of *constraints,* and the verbal *speech* or discourse of the officer. A rhetorical situation can be SIMPLE or COMPLEX, depending on the number of elements involved. Bitzer defines a SIMPLE situation as one in which a few elements have to be made to interact. For our purposes, an officer who finds himself dealing with a single individual in an alley, with few or no bystanders, is in a SIMPLE rhetorical situation. That same officer, faced with four or five suspects verbally assaulting him and demanding attention while numerous bystanders shout and give advice, is in a COMPLEX situation, for he must attempt to make numerous elements and forces interact if he is to be successful at resolving the crisis.

Obviously, if the rhetorical situation is COMPLEX and the officer fails to read it as such, he can cause more trouble than he initially had. If he acts as if the scene is SIMPLE, he will ignore problems and individuals who should be addressed, thus angering people he need not have angered or possibly even endangering his own life by failing to recognize the explosive potential in the scene. Such is the officer who fails to make distinctions between victims and perpetrators as he speaks, making the victims feel somehow guilty and responsible for what happened to them and the perpetrators feel important. Such is the officer who fails to consider relevant "extenuating circumstances" in making a decision to arrest or not to arrest. Such is the officer who, in trying to arbitrate a domestic dispute, turns his back on the wife while he berates the angered husband, inviting an attack by the suddenly protective wife.

Conversely, an officer who mistakes a SIMPLE rhetorical encounter for a COMPLEX one can cause problems and endanger his own life. Such is the officer who, called to a fight scene in a parking lot on a main street, arrives ready to arrest or hassle everyone in the lot rather than address the single exigency or problem that led to the call. To mistake bystanders for troublemakers is often to enlarge a problem, which may turn a simple encounter into a complex one.

The skill needed in all scenes, whether SIMPLE or COMPLEX, is to be capable of recognizing the real exigency or problem(s), the appropriate audience, and the actual set of constraints involved in the scene. Only when these elements are correctly seen and evaluated can an officer *create* the appropriate verbal response.

Structure of Rhetorical Scenes

Professor Bitzer also points out that a rhetorical scene can be highly structured or loosely structured (391). A HIGHLY STRUCTURED scene is one in which all the elements "are located and readied for the task to be performed" (391). Bitzer uses the courtroom case as an example of a COMPLEX and HIGHLY STRUCTURED rhetorical situation because all elements — the jury, the legal counsels, the judge, the law, the defendant, and sometimes even the evidence — are clear and well defined. The participants know their jobs and their relationships to one another. A SIMPLE but HIGHLY STRUCTURED situation might be the booking of a suspect, for in this case the steps are clear and prescribed and thus

HIGHLY STRUCTURED, yet the officer has to deal with only a single individual and relatively few rhetorical problems or constraints.

But the most usual rhetorical scene in police work is the LOOSELY STRUCTURED scene — SIMPLE or COMPLEX. Street scenes are usually made up of unpredictable variables and complex factors. The officer who attempts to disperse a crowd or quell a riot faces a COMPLEX but LOOSELY STRUCTURED situation, for he must search for effective arguments or appeals and sometimes even for a genuine rhetorical audience, one capable of being influenced or moved by words. He may, in fact, have to create an audience by the force of his personality and style. Admittedly, police procedure can sometimes provide the officer with the means to turn a loosely structured scene into a highly structured one, as in the arrest of a DWI suspect or the emergency evacuation of personnel during a bomb threat. Even with police procedure, however, an officer will have to improvise and add his own structuring principles to most scenes (an issue we will explore in detail in Chapter 6, "Organization").

For now, it is important to understand that any rhetorical situation can be *weakened* in structure by two factors: complexity or disconnectedness. As Professor Bitzer describes it, a rhetorical situation can be weakened by numerous causes, three of which are crucial in police work:

1. A single rhetorical situation may have *numerous* exigencies or problems.
2. Two or more rhetorical situations may *compete* for the officer's attention.
3. In any one scene, persons comprising the audience of situation A may also be the audience for situations B, C, and D (pp. 391-392).

Each of these *threats* to the rhetorical situation can be lessened by the skillful and aware officer who is capable of seeing and bringing his command presence to the scene.

Consider, for example, the *first* instance, where you face several exigencies or problems in a single situation. Your task, which will have to be performed almost instantaneously, will be to *assess* the competing rhetorical problems and *select* one to serve as the central or organizing one. The *degree* of severity of each problem and the *probability* of your ability to affect it by means of verbal persuasion, rather than force, will be your best criteria for making your decision. A fight in progress is more severe than a fight about to begin, *unless* you note, for example, that weapons are part of the second exigency. On the other hand, if you are called to a scene outside a tavern and, as you arrive, you note that two people are wrestling around on the sidewalk, surrounded by highly vocal and intoxicated bystanders, which problem would you address first? Probably it would be dangerous to address the sidewalk brawl *before* getting the agitated crowd back away from the scene. To plunge through the crowd to get to the pair on the sidewalk might result in a third exigency: *you* getting attacked by the onlookers.

If the first rhetorical situation deals with competing exigencies within a single situation, the second one concerns two different rhetorical situations within one encounter scene. For example, in a domestic dispute the officer may well have to face two *different* rhetorical situations as he attempts to deal first with the wife, then with her husband. His skill as an arbiter will partly depend on his ability to respond in a *fitting* way to the two different speakers and their emotional needs. He may have to *be* two different persons alternately: one to handle the wife, another to handle the husband. One set of appeals and dialogue might work with one party but not with the other. In essence, then, although the encounter scene is singular (one call to one house), the rhetorical demands may be multiple. The officer's goal will be either to negotiate successfully with each party separately or to make both parties come together in a third rhetorical scene that is controlled and directed by the officer himself. Using this latter approach, the officer might lead the subjects to see that the largest problem (living peacefully together) cannot be solved in isolation; that is, each subject must make concessions and help to build new bridges of communication. The "trick" or verbal judo here, in this instance, involves moving the subjects to see beyond the immediate areas of controversy into the more general area of shared values and goals.

In other words, one mark of the skillful patrol officer is his ability to MAKE a new rhetorical situation out of two or more competing situations. To be able to do this efficiently, however, the officer must first be capable of recognizing competing rhetorical scenes as just that — competing *scenes*. He must then be capable of *transforming* those scenes into a new configuration or entity that he can control and direct.

In a domestic dispute, for example, the officer has been called to act as a "third party," one whose business it is to break a locked emotional situation and modify the behaviors of the participants. As the new element in the scene, then, the officer has the ability (even the duty) to alter the situation dramatically by making himself the crucial audience. This change in the rhetorical elements can transform the situation significantly enough to open new lines of communication and inquiry that have previously been closed. His own discourse or talk becomes the second crucial element new to the scene, and by it he can begin to move the subjects towards some kind of resolution.

Taking charge of a situation, then, mainly means *remaking* or newly *creating* rhetorical scenes. The *third* threat to the rhetorical situation also demands that the officer take charge using the technique of *re-creation*. When an officer faces a scene in which he has *competing audiences* already in the scene vying for the subject's attention, he has a problem. Consider a street scene in which four teenagers have been vandalizing a vehicle belonging to a family despised by others in the neighborhood. As the officer arrives, a crowd of approving neighbors gathers in the street and urges the vandals on.

The officer entering such a scene encounters a very complex and potentially explosive rhetorical situation. The vandals are playing to the encouragement of the crowd; perhaps, also, they are responding to the angry protests of the owners. Additionally, the vandals are playing and responding to each other's urgings and expectations. Typically, kids in trouble play to one another; they serve each other as audiences, daring and encouraging one another.

The officer readily sees that his main audience will be the vandals; it is to them that he must speak and exert his authority. But he also sees that he has other audiences to deal with: the crowd of neighbors in the street, the angry victims, and the boys as they play audience for each other. If he is to be successful in controlling the encounter, the officer is going to have to make himself the primary audience and minimize the effect of the other competing audiences. One mistake the officer must not make is to regard this street scene as a SIMPLE rhetorical situation, for it is clearly COMPLEX. If he sees the problem of multiple audience, he will recognize the scene's complexity and make fewer errors in dealing with it.

He will, for example, understand that some of the emotional energy in the actions of the vandals is precipitated by the scene itself, the multiple audiences noted. The skillful officer will use his energies not in overreaction but in methodically going about the business of remaking the situation to fit his immediate purposes. One way to begin such a transformation, of course, would be to disperse the gathered crowd before confronting the subjects. Or, perhaps, he will choose to neutralize the subjects first and then get rid of the bystanders, including the victims who should return to their home and await police contact. Or, again, he might decide to neutralize the subjects and select one or two bystanders as witnesses. Then, keeping the victims of the vandalism present and clearing the area of all other persons not necessary to the scene, he can begin to move towards resolution of the problem by making himself the single audience for those left in the area; they must respond to him, no one else. His command presence now directs the entire scene, from beginning to end.

In the *three threats* to the structure of any rhetorical scene, we have seen how important it is for the street officer to be AWARE of the scene as a structured entity that can be broken at any point. The major causes of break — multiple problems, competing rhetorical situations, and competing audiences — can be avoided if the officer thinks in terms of modifying or transforming a scene, changing its physical state. Whenever an officer fails to change prevailing rhetorical states, such states threaten to cease becoming rhetorical, open to verbal persuasion, and instead become scenes of violence and physical force. Rhetorical situations, then, can collapse or degenerate, and when they do, the officer has little choice but to use force or retreat. Since all human encounters change as they progress in time, it is important for the street officer to be in control of such changes rather than to be controlled by them. Knowing the threats to a rhetorical situation, as well as knowing the elements of one, can give an officer the power to keep control during one.

The "Life" of a Rhetorical Situation

Rhetorical situations are brought to life by problems that invite verbal persuasion. They can mature or decay, depending on the officer's responses to them. Professor Bitzer writes that rhetorical situations "evolve to a time when rhetorical discourse is most fitting" (1971, p. 392). After this moment, Bitzer suggests, the rhetorical situation will decay. We have all been in situations where we have said, "If only I had said what I had to say at *that point,* things would have turned out better than they did." The "if-only-I-had-thought-of-that-then" phrase is common to all of us and it points to what Bitzer calls the "life" of a rhetorical situation.

Rhetorical situations, then, call for a response, but not just any response. It should be a *fitting response,* one which clearly meets the requirements of the situation. Situations that are rhetorical *call for* certain kinds of responses, and it is necessary for police officers to READ scenes in terms of what kinds of responses are fitting and proper and what are not. Many street scenes are strong and clear scenes, ones which almost dictate the proper police response, in terms of purpose, "theme," matter, and style of response. Others, such as the ones we have described previously, are not as clear or strong, and these need the officer to shape or transform them into scenes that he can handle using words as his major tool.

Now that we have analyzed what a rhetorical situation is, defined its types, described its structure, and suggested its potential to mature and decay, we can turn to one of the crucial components of a rhetorical situation, AUDIENCE, and describe some ways an officer can analyze his audience and make fitting responses to it.

TYPES OF AUDIENCES

The police officer meets six different kinds of audiences during his work and each type has its own problems and demands.

Type 1: The Single Person, Well Defined and Known

Type 1 is an audience in every police officer's day; it is the single individual who is *known* by the officer because of repeated contact. It may be the local businessman or the habitual offender, but it is someone with whom the officer has grown accustomed to dealing with and therefore someone he knows fairly well. Often, this audience is the easiest to encounter because the officer knows generally what to expect from the subject and which kinds of strategies or ploys work and which do not. Such knowledge usually makes the rhetorical response of the officer clear-cut, but the danger lies in assuming that the subject will respond in a given instance as he has in the past. Although the officer may expect the subject to behave in predictable ways, he should always be ready for an abrupt change, due to some variable unknown to the officer.

Type 2: The Single Person, Unknown

As in the above case, the officer faces an audience of one, but this time the individual is *unknown,* a fact which poses some difficulties. Given the precise nature of the street encounter, the officer may acquire some knowledge of this unknown subject. Aside from the details of clothing, physical description, and distinctive mannerisms, the officer may pick up clues concerning his subject from what the subject was *doing* when the officer encountered him and how he speaks at the scene. The immediate situation may make it clear whether the subject is victim, bystander, or perpetrator, but often it will not. There may be doubt and ambiguity concerning the status of the subject. The officer will have to evaluate his subject by reading signs (verbal and non-verbal clues) and use those clues in communicating with the subject.

The one-on-one encounter may appear simple, but it can be most complex. Whenever two people converse, there are at least six "selves" complicating the process.

The Officer	The Other Individual
1. The real self (buried)	1. The real self (buried)
2. Officer as he sees himself	2. Subject as he sees himself
3. Officer as seen by subject	3. Subject as seen by the officer

The problem of communicating with someone else is deepened by the chances of misreading either oneself or the other person. Where there exists a conflict between how the officer sees himself (level two) and how he is seen by the other (level three), miscommunication is bound to occur. The officer may see himself as rational and flexible, but the subject may see him as overbearing and overconfident. Such conflict may arise because of something actually said or done by the officer or because of some deep-rooted prejudice or bias of the subject. A citizen's perspective can be clouded by bias just as easily as an officer's, a problem we examined in the last chapter.

Likewise, where there exists a conflict between how the citizen sees himself (level two) and how he is seen by the officer (level three), communication problems will occur. The subject may see himself as rational and entirely within his rights, but the officer may see him as unreasonable or suspicious, given his reading of the scene and the nature of the call, should there have been one.

Whenever there is a difference in the way two people respond to the image of the other, there will be communication problems. The officer, since he must assume control and direct the encounter, must be alert to such differences and attempt to modify or change the subject's view of the situation, which includes altering the subject's view of the officer.

Type 3: Single Group, Well Defined

An officer's street world is made up of several well-known groups: the teen gangs that hang around on corners and parking lots, the neighborhood groups, and special interest clans of all kinds. In each case, the officer generally finds himself dealing with the same group repeatedly and he handles them as a single group. Even a known family that has repeated domestic disputes, usually about the same issue or issues, fits in this category. From experience, the officer knows to treat the individuals involved as a group and he knows the group's perspective and usual mode of response. Thus, he tailors his communication to fit the entity rather than the single member. The same danger, of course, exists here as in Type 1: overconfidence in technique and approach.

Type 4: The Single Group, Unknown

The single group, unknown, poses severe problems for the officer, for he must decide whether to treat the group as a group or attempt to isolate those individuals within the group who can influence the others to go the way the officer wants. Those who understand the complexity of just two people talking together (the six "selves" that conflict with one another) can appreciate the added difficulty of trying to communicate with an unknown group of individuals. The potential for misunderstanding and making rhetorical blunders is great; the officer must attempt to read the group well enough to determine what approach and voice would be most effective. He must determine whether to speak to the leaders, should he be able to spot them, or to address the group as a group, attempting to establish some kind of rapport with it. Whatever approach he takes will be partly based on other exigencies — time, weather, and the nature of the call — and partly based on the results of his reading the behavioral clues of the group. He must see, evaluate, and then adopt a manner that he believes will achieve his purposes. He must, in other words, make *known* the *unknown* group as quickly as possible.

Type 5: Multiple Groups, Well Defined

Two or more street gangs, two or more families in a dispute, or two or more groups in a street demonstration are examples of multiple groups. If the officer has previous knowledge and experience with these groups, they are *known* entities and belong in this category. Dealing with multiple groups is never easy, but if the officer knows each group, he has some insight into how the various groups are likely to react (to each other and to him) and he can begin the task of interacting with them by using what he does know. If he has experience of this audience, he will know what rhetorical strategies to try and what not, but he may know only each group as an audience and find himself encountering them as a mixed audience for the first time. If so, he will have to use what he knows about each group to assess the best probable approach to them as a mixture, which he does not yet know. The rule of thumb here is to have the officer use what he does *know* to discover what he does *not know*, namely, how to appeal to the multiple groups as an entity.

Type 6: Multiple Groups, Unknown

This last is the most difficult of all, for the unknowns are many and the potential for failure is great. Again, the crucial task for the officer as he enters the situation is to determine the nature of the exigency, the problem, and to decide whether to treat the several groups as one entity or as several. If he decides on the latter course of action, he has to decide whether to isolate leaders in each group and address them or to address the several groups as single entities with a common problem. His ability to "size up" the audience, to read it, will depend on his perception of the rhetorical situation and on his capability to note clues and to assess their meaning.

Just to be able to perceive that a gathering of people is actually a mixture of several "groups" is a necessary beginning. Then to be able to identify from given behavioral clues the mixture of definable groups is the next necessary step. In other words, once an audience is seen by the officer as consisting of definable groups with certain definable traits, he is in a position to make rhetorical decisions concerning what appeal or strategy that should be used.

I have sketched the six most common audiences for the street officer. Any mixture of types will, of course, further complicate the communication process. For example, an officer may confront a mixture of Type 1 and Type 2 when he confronts one individual he knows and one he does not at the same time. When this happens, the officer must take care not to assume that well-known B will respond in predictable ways given the presence of unknown C. The unknown individual C may be just the variable to make B unpredictable.

No matter what audience is at hand, it is important for the officer to regard audience analysis as crucial to his success. He must think of those he confronts in his daily work as AUDIENCES, single or multiple entities that can be defined and influenced. The officer must often be the director of a street scene, much like a director of a stage play, and he must also play the part of actor, one whose job it is to influence the audience in certain ways. Whether director or actor, or both simultaneously, the officer must *know* his audience as well as he possibly can. The section that follows offers several techniques that can sharpen an officer's ability to make on-the-street analyses of audience.

TECHNIQUES TO ANALYZE AN AUDIENCE

I. Projection and Identification with an Audience

Whether an officer faces a single individual or a group, one useful control technique is to see the situation from the other person's (or group's) point of view. If the officer remains open and flexible, maintaining his *disinterest,* he will be capable of such "double vision." The double vision allows the officer to see through the eyes of another. Often when an officer contacts a citizen, the latter is upset or overwrought about some problem he wants the officer to solve. Or, equally possibly, the citizen doesn't want the officer anywhere near the situation. Whatever the case, the citizen has his point of view, right or wrong, just or unjust.

For an officer to bring order out of disorder, sense out of nonsense, he must understand the street problem and control if not solve it. Whenever a street problem is rhetorical (that is, whenever it can be managed by verbal persuasion), the officer's best strategy is to attempt to see the problem from the point of view of the citizen involved. Momentarily, then, the officer suspends judgment and tries imaginatively to see as the other sees. To do this, the officer must *identify* with the other; he must put himself in the place of the other and look at the situation through the eyes of the subject.

To be able to *suspend judgment* is the first crucial step. If you, as officer, withhold judgments and conclusions long enough to hear the other out and listen to his story, you can gather sufficient material to read the scene as the subject does. The more material you can gather, the better your opportunity to understand the situation completely and resolve it. You do not have to agree with anything the other says, you simply have to understand your subject's particular perspective. If you withhold judgments, you can *project* yourself imaginatively into the other, seeing the world as he sees it. Such projection may result in sympathy, understanding, even agreement, but it need not. It need only give you a fuller and surer sense of your subject, your audience, and his particular problem. In short, *suspension of judgment* and *projection* are practical street aids because they increase your chances of discovering fitting rhetorical *means* to solve the street problem.

Admittedly, some officers will possess more imagination and "projective power" than others, but there are three basic, necessary steps that all officers can take that will improve their ability to "know" an unknown subject. First, officers should understand *what kind of relations can exist between X and themselves*. In any given police call or street scene, the possible personal relationships between officer and subject will vary. In some scenes, the officer can see the potential for considerable give and take of communication, for real reciprocal communication. In other scenes, because of the nature of the problem, the communication process will have to be mostly one way: from officer to subject. Whatever the case, the officer must anticipate the *kind* of communication potential present in each scene right from the beginning. If the scene, for example, seems to warrant several warnings, explanations, or some kind of "teaching," then the officer faces a different kind of scene than if these potential purposes were absent.

The second step to knowing X is to know through experience what it is like *to stand in approximate relations to things of the kind that X is*. When handling a domestic dispute call, for example, an officer can draw upon his own experience of emotional conflict to recall what it is like to be in such a situation. The very act of recalling a similar situation in one's own life generates sufficient emotional and mental understanding to appreciate, even if not approve, the actions and viewpoint of the subject. The officer who says, "I've been there; I know what you mean," has taken this step. He remembers what it is like to have been governed by rage, and he can thus speak to the subject with increased understanding and emotional awareness. He has "projected into the other," if only for a moment. The art of street sense and street negotiation is largely a matter of such "approximation;" difference is not stressed, similarity is, and it is within the "approximate" area of experience that the officer can find his means for more skillful communication.

The third step to knowing X is *to identify the role that X is playing and stand in relation to that role*. Although not all human behavior is role playing, much is, and when one wishes to identify with another, for whatever the purposes, it is necessary to define the other person's present role and attempt to relate specifically to it. Many persons who an officer comes in contact with during a working shift are playing out roles, often roles of which they are not clearly aware. The earlier example of the man who holds a knife to the throat of his young son and plans to kill him because he believes the boy has been possessed by a devil is playing the role of the avenging angel, the cleanser of evil, and he sees himself in the light of this role. Indeed, the role, once adopted, may force the subject to do things that he would not ever do otherwise. In other words, roles have a force of their own; people change given the roles that they adopt.

The officer who understands the power of roles and who can adjust his talk according to the role adopted by the subject has markedly improved his ability to "identify" with the subject. Moreover, having understood the role of the subject, the officer is now in a position to adopt an appropriate counter-role that may effectively communicate to the subject. Role harmony rather than role conflict is the goal here.

The three steps — (1) knowing what kinds of relations can exist between officer and subject, (2) knowing the approximate relations to things as X knows them, and (3) knowing X's role and standing in relation to that role — can improve an officer's ability to project into another's emotional and perceptual world for the purposes of communicating or controlling his behavior. Some officers have a "knack" of relating to others, but all of us can improve our ability if we attempt to take the three steps described. These steps can help you make accurate *inferences* about the subject you face and adjust your role accordingly. The ability to look through the eyes of your subject will give you a surer sense of what he knows, how he feels, and what his present needs may be at the moment — all crucial signs of how he may be influenced or moved. If you can accurately assess how a subject sees himself and the world around him, you can more surely evaluate how he will respond to the possible options that you might offer him.

Just as crucially, *suspension of judgment* and *projection and identification* enable officers to discover a language and a voice to speak to a subject. To know the peculiar view of a subject is to anticipate what actions and what words may set him off into violence. What might be a "trigger" word for one subject might not be for another. As officer, you may decide on a "message," a meaning to convey to the subject, but there are numerous ways the same message can be delivered. Whenever we speak, we *encode* our meaning in words, symbols, and the listener has to *decode* our message to get our meaning. Depending on how well we have understood our audience, we will more or less effectively encode our meaning for our subject, who must decode it.

Although we will examine this encoding and decoding process in fuller depth in the next chapter, "Voice," it is important to sketch the communication process here. Examine the following diagram.

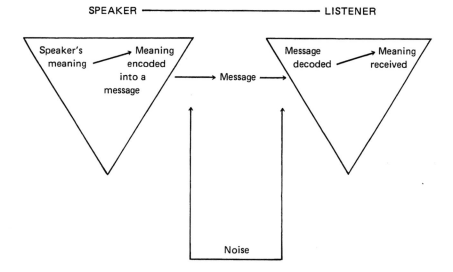

This communications model was developed by electrical engineers during World War II, who were trying to increase the amount of information transmitted through such electronic equipment as radios and telephones. Their model depicts the speaker as a combination of a radio announcer and a transmitter who sends his message out on airwaves.

In the model, the speaker has to encode his message in some form that will accurately express his meaning. We saw in the chapter on "Perspective" how easy it is to load our messages with bias. Moreover, once the message is sent to the receiver (i.e. the subject on the street), there are numerous "noises" that can interfere in the transmission. "Noise" can refer to things such as actual noise in the street

— a crowd shouting or sirens wailing — or to the sender's poor organization, illogic, or obviously biased attitudes.

Once the receiver, the subject, gets the message, he must attempt to decode it back into *meaning*. Since this is an interpretive matter, "noise" can again have an effect. The subject may be confused, angry, or just plain tired, and any one of these physical states may be enough for him to miss crucial words in the message or obvious intentions. Whatever his state, the subject will not remember what you *tell* him as much as he will remember what he *tells himself*. He will make *inferences* based on what he believes you said and meant; he will, in other words, *make his own meaning* from what you have said. He will be *creative*, not passive, in decoding your message and he will use whatever he knows, believes, or expects to arrive at an understanding of what you meant.

Therefore, it is very important that you anticipate his view of the world, see through his eyes, before you make your own verbal message. The better you have analyzed your audience, the better your chances of saying what you must in language that will be decoded or understood the way you wish it to be. To become one with your audience, momentarily and imaginatively, is to decrease greatly the chances of rhetorical blunders occasioned by poor encoding. One good guideline is, don't encode until you know to whom you're sending the message, and in order to "know" you must first see as the other. Once you have taken this necessary step, you are ready to *shape* your own presence or "character" to meet the subject's expectations and needs and to put your message into language that will be readily and accurately understood. Like an actor, then, you should suit your character to the script and demands of the scene, but unlike the actor, you must make your own script from the materials of the scene and, particularly, from the evidence that you receive from your audience analysis.

II. The Rogerian Approach to Communication

Carl R. Rogers, a psychotherapist, has developed a communication strategy that offers a valid alternative to the traditional argumentative-persuasive approach. It is particularly useful in situations of powerful conflict, where commitments to values are strong and emotions run high. All types of managers of aggressive behavior — police officers, parole officers, social workers, juvenile officers, corrections personnel, or psychotherapists — can profit from the strategy for persuasion outlined by Carl Rogers. In cases of high tension or emotionalism, logical argument rarely has much effect. As police officers, you will often work in the "hot" area of communications; that is, you will often have to attempt to modify or change someone's behavior in an atmosphere of extreme pressure. Any number of rhetorical strategies are possible, but the Rogers model can serve as one basic approach from which variations can be created as the street situation permits.

The Rogers model supposes that there are three main obstacles to communication:

1. Threats hinder communication. When a subject feels threatened by what the officer is saying, he is likely to stop listening in order to protect his ego and reduce anxiety.
2. Strong statements of opinion stimulate an audience to respond similarly. Once strong opinions have been voiced, people tend to defend them rather than discuss them.
3. Biased language increases the sense of threat; neutral language reduces it.*

Using the skills of *suspension of judgment* and *projection,* the Rogerian model emphasizes *empathy* between the speaker and the listener, or, in our case, the officer's ability to see as the other sees. In fact, the first step in Rogerian communication is to convey to the subject that he is *understood.*

STEP 1: Let the audience know its position is understood. By "understood," Rogers means to see the issue and attitude from the other person's point of view, to sense how he feels about it by understanding his frame of reference and context. This step requires the *disinterest* we have defined earlier and it requires the *projection* of self into the other. If you encounter an angry subject on a call and take the time to see the problem as he sees it and then attempt to restate in your own words the subject's position, taking care not to judge it, you have taken the first Rogerian step. Most subjects are accus-

---

*Rogers, Carl: *On Becoming a Person* (Boston: Houghton-Mifflin Company, 1961), pp. 329 – 337.

tomed to hearing the officer's view of the problem first; to present the subject with an unbiased restatement of his own position is to capture his attention (he will listen to see if you have correctly stated it) and to reduce the sense of threat that he most probably feels. In this way, you can encourage him to pursue discussion of his own position, perhaps to reconsider his position, and even change it.

STEP 2: State the contexts within which the subject's position is (or might be) valid or acceptable. In traditional argument, people try to point out defects or weaknesses in another's position; but in Rogerian strategy you focus on the positive or valid thoughts of the subject. This further reduces his sense of threat and offers further evidence that his position is understood. What is right or not right, valid or invalid, is usually a matter of *context;* if you, the officer, are aware of the importance of context in matters of differing opinion, you can more readily understand opposing positions and accept disagreement with your own position. People "edit" experience in different ways and hence facts, opinions, and beliefs will have greater or lesser weight depending on who is observing what in the given situation.

Because citizens are often ignorant or unclear of the law governing a given situation, it is most helpful if the officer attempts to outline the strong points of the subject's perspective before pointing out its weaknesses. Show the subject the limits inside of which he is right rather than the limits outside of which he is wrong. Cooperation is made much more likely, then, because you have lessened the threat to the subject.

STEP 3: State the contexts in which your position, as officer, is valid or acceptable. It is here that you describe to the subject the reason you are on the scene and how you see the situation now, given what he has said. One of the values of doing Step 1 and Step 2 first, before giving your own position, is that these steps may make the subject more *receptive* to hearing your side of things. You, after all, have listened to his side and have attempted to state it accurately. Now you can define the issue as you see it because you have created an atmosphere of provisional problem solving and trust. The rhetorical strategy has created a situation of reciprocity: "I listened to you; now hear my side."

In other words, often you will have to *re-create* your audience before you can persuade or alter his perceptions. An angry or confused person is not likely to be a receptive audience initially. What you have to do, using verbal strategy, is to *remake* him as audience. Steps 1 – 3 can help you do just this because, by first making it appear that you care about his position, you can induce in him the similar response. If you behave *as if* he is capable of listening to your view as carefully as you listened to his, the chances are improved that he will respond as you expect.

Most important in this step is your attempt to outline the areas in which you and the subject *agree;* the more you can show the subject that the two of you *share* attitudes, experiences, or values, the greater your chance of getting compliance from him. Looking for bridges of communication, shared perspectives, or attitudes is one of the signs of a good negotiator, a skillful conflict resolver. To stress that which you share with each other rather than how you differ is to increase the chances of trust and cooperation and minimize conflict. The officer who says to a subject who has been discovered urinating in public, "I know what it's like to have to piss and to have no place to go to do it — I've been there — but the alleyway would have been far more appropriate than this corner," stands a good chance of defusing what could become an explosive situation. Police officers always run the danger of appearing to their public as moral paragons of virtue, and anything an officer can do to appear more "human" and understanding will greatly increase his chances of succeeding without violence.

STEP 4: Show how the audience would benefit from accepting your position. In all street scenes, there comes a time for the officer to make his will felt, to direct the subject and to resolve the problem. Normally, this means the subject must bend to the officer's will (rarely is it the other way), but if Steps 1 – 3 have been taken first, the subject's resistance is likely to be far less than otherwise. Moreover, if the officer has taken Steps 1 – 3, he is likely to discover a more workable solution to the problem than otherwise. Knowing the subject's perspective, knowing its acceptable limits, and having discovered shared areas of relationship all permit the officer to make the most appropriate and sensitive resolution. Often, some rule of law will determine the final solution; at other times, the particular circumstances of the street encounter will determine the outcome. In many cases, both the law and the unique circumstances will determine resolution. But whatever the case, if the officer can demonstrate that his solution to the street problem recognizes the interests of *all parties,* he stands to succeed with fewer problems and repercussions than the officer who only stresses his own interests.

There exist really four possible kinds of solutions in terms of final results. The first is the WIN-LOSE solution. In this resolution, the police officer WINS and the subject LOSES. The subject loses face and the argument. The second kind of resolution is the LOSE-LOSE condition; in this case, the officer loses and the subject loses. An instance of this might be a scene in which an officer, through the use of force and will, arrests a troublemaker but, because of the way he handles the situation, loses respect and confidence from those witnessing the event.

The most dangerous and clearly the worst kind of resolution is the LOSE-WIN situation. In this instance, an officer, either because of procedure or behavior, LOSES the street confrontation with the subject. The subject WINS something, either in his eyes or in others', and the officer LOSES something, either in his eyes or in others'. Such a case might be when an officer makes an arrest but loses the case in court because of his poor handling of the situation, either in terms of procedure or personal behavior. The officer loses both the case and his reputation and the subject walks, regardless of how guilty he may have been.

The fourth possibility is clearly the best. The WIN-WIN situation. In the final resolution of the street encounter, the officer WINS something and the subject WINS something. In some way or another, both parties have been satisfied. Even in situations in which the end result is the arrest of the subject — the officer WINS — if the officer has handled the scene in such a manner that the subject can save face or maintain some kind of dignity, the subject WINS also. Because so much of police work entails bending the will of others to conform to the law, the way in which this is handled makes a great deal of difference to those coerced. It also makes a real difference to the patrol officer, for his ultimate reputation and power depends on how well he can skillfully manage other people's behavior.

One real value of the model for communication proposed by

Carl Rogers, then, is its stress on the WIN-WIN communication situation. It provides direction for audience analysis and for persuasion, but it works from totally different premises than traditional argument, which stresses the WIN-LOSE perspective and the PRO vs. the CON. Rogerian argument guides people to create situations conducive to cooperation; for the street officer it provides a specific means to generate two-way traffic, the give and take of communication between sender and receiver, cop and subject. Even more than its specific strategies, however, Rogerian rhetoric is an attitude, a HABIT OF MIND, that can create and sustain channels of communication that might otherwise be destroyed or weakened by the more traditional approach. In this sense, then, it is highly practical and efficacious.

SUMMARY

In this chapter you have seen that rhetorical situations are those in which verbal persuasion is a workable means to resolving conflict. The four elements of a rhetorical situation are (1) a problem or exigency, (2) an audience that has to be addressed, (3) a set of constraints that hinder persuasion, and (4) your own speech or discourse, together with your personality and style.

You have also seen that rhetorical situations can be simple or complex: they are simple if you have few elements which have to be made to relate and they are complex if you have many. Moreover, rhetorical situations have a structure. They will be loose if they have many variable and unpredictable relationships; they will be highly structured if all the elements and relationships in the situation are clear and well defined.

Further, rhetorical situations can weaken or break down if at least one of the following three causes exist: (1) numerous problems within one situation, (2) two or more rhetorical situations compete for the officer's attention, or (3) if there are multiple and competing audiences that have to be faced. Add to these "threats" the fact that rhetorical scenes have a "life cycle" of their own, which means that they can grow and mature or decay and die depending on the officer's response to them.

Rhetorical skill, then, is partly dependent on a clear understanding of the rhetorical situation, its elements, and its structure in any given case. Because rhetoric is situational, so much will depend on your ability to analyze the immediate occasion and create a suitable response to its particulars.

One of the crucial "particulars" in the rhetorical situation is AUDIENCE, and much of your success in dealing with street people will be a result of your ability to define an audience and to play to it. We looked at *six* different types of audiences, which ranged from the single individual to the mixed groups, known and unknown. We then explored two approaches to dealing with people in the rhetorical situation: (1) projection and identification and (2) Rogerian rhetoric. In the first approach, we discussed some general and specific characteristics of the approach (disinterest, suspension of judgment, and projection) and we explored three steps conducive to developing the proper mental and emotional states to see a situation through the eyes of another. In the second approach (the Rogerian process), we identified four distinct steps that could create a climate of give and take, even of trust. Both approaches rest on the assumption that communication is a matter of an *action/reaction* chain, which is the main motive force. Moreover, because communication is also a matter of encoding and decoding, both approaches insist on a basic attitude of sensitivity to the other person's context and point of view. Messages can go wrong at any number of points; they can be misunderstood because of the way we put them, the way we encode our meaning. They can also be decoded wrongly because of external "noise" or because of the internal state of the decoder (physical, mental, or emotional).

Lastly, both approaches imply that who we are at any given moment depends partly on the situation in which we find ourselves and partly on the actions we take. In other words, character or "self" grows out of action. *We make ourselves into what we have to become to relate effectively to the events, circumstances, personalities, and actions of others as we find them in the rhetorical encounter scene.* What we say and what we do is determined by our response to the demands of the particular situation. Thinking of reaction in these terms, we run far less risk of being "rigid" or inflexible or being misunderstood as such. We can be firm yet open, ready for the twists and turns of the verbal encounter.

Sensitivity to audience, then, is not a weak nor soft way to deal with people; it is, in fact, the crucial element in the art of resolving potentially dangerous street encounters using appropriate words and strategies. It gives us POWER when we need it.

MINI-CASES ON AUDIENCE ANALYSIS

General Directions

Read each case through twice to become familiar with the details. For each case, determine whether it is an overall success or failure, then do the following:

1. Determine the EXIGENCY or problem in each.
2. List as precisely as you can the SET OF CONSTRAINTS that the officer has to work with.
3. Analyze the AUDIENCE in each. List crucial traits the officer recognized or responded to or failed to note.
4. Describe as clearly as you can the officer's PERSPECTIVE in the opening of the scene. Are biases reflected in how he handles the situation?
5. Try to pinpoint as accurately as you can precisely where the officer begins to make mistakes or clearly avoids mistakes. What rhetorical strategies were used?
6. Consider the "larger implications" of the strategies used. Would the successful techniques pictured here *always* work? Usually fail?
7. Be prepared to offer an alternative approach to handling the problem.

Case 1: "Domestic Dispute"

Cast: *Wife*
Husband
Two children, upstairs (They have come down twice, crying, and are upstairs trying to go to sleep.)
Officer Adams and Officer Clay

Scene: *Two officers are called to a residence where the couple have been yelling and shouting at one another for over thirty minutes. Sounds of violence from the home have caused neighbors to call the police. Officers meet subjects on porch. Subjects are yelling at each other on porch.*

Officer Adams *(Walking up to the husband and wife, holding up his hand):* Okay, okay, let's calm down, now. The neighbors have complained about the noise here. What seems to be the problem?

Wife: This son of a bitch has been pushing me around for hours. He always comes home late for dinner and then yells at me for not having something on the table!

Husband: That's a lot of bullshit! She always accuses me of staying in a bar and drinking, but I've been looking for a job. That's why I'm usually late!

Wife: Job, hell! You've found nothing to do for over two months, ever since you got out of the army. *(To officers)* He thinks because he was in Viet Nam he's a big deal. People owe him, that's his view. He doesn't really try, and then when he doesn't get a job he comes home and takes it out on me and the kids! And, hell, I work eight hours a day!

Husband: Yeah, that's all I ever hear, how hard she works! She's the savior of the family and I'm the bad guy! *(Slams his fist into his hand)*

Officer Adams: All right, enough, enough! Do you have children upstairs, sir?

Husband: Yeah, my two boys.

Wife: Hey, they're mine, too, you bastard! See, that's his problem! Everything is his. What an ego!

Officer Clay: I'll tell you what, ma'am; why don't you step over here with me and let Officer Adams here have a chat with your husband. We're not getting anywhere shouting back and forth. *(Officer Clay and woman go off to one side)*

Officer Adams: In Viet Nam, huh? How long?

Husband: Four years, in and out of combat. Then I spent six months in a VA hospital while they worked on this right arm, here. *(Pats his arm)* It's still not 100 percent, but it's getting there. But I'm looking for factory work and all the bastards do is raise a question whether I can handle the physical work. Each employer wants to see my entire medical history, so I've written off for it, but it all takes time and meanwhile my bitch here keeps yapping! *(Gestures towards woman)*

Officer Adams: Yeah, I can understand your frustration. But, look, what about your kids upstairs? Don't you think all this yelling and screaming with your wife frightens them?

Husband: Yeah, that really makes me madder at her. They've been down twice tonight crying. They're *my boys!*

Officer Adams: But they are hers, too, right? Do you really think that it's worth all their pain to get back at her?

Husband: Not when you put it like that, I guess. But, Jesus, she doesn't know how to treat a man, always bitching and howling, and she doesn't even know what the hell I've been trying to do!

Officer Adams: Have you told her? I mean, really sat down and explained why you are having the problems with the employers, about the demands for medical records, and all the questions about your health? Have you really let her in on it as it *really* is?

Husband: Hell, no, a man's got to handle some things on his own! I tried once to describe the problem, but she was too upset about me being late to dinner — a big thirty minutes late, too. Big fucking deal!

Officer Adams: To her, maybe, but then again it might not be so big a deal if you told her the whole story and shared your frustration with her instead of shielding her from it. I bet she's tough enough to understand it; hell, she'd probably transfer her anger at those employers rather than you. Then you two would kind of be in it together, don't you think?

Husband: I guess you've got a point there. All this battling ain't getting us very far anyway, except it's hurting the kids.

Officer Adams: Well, okay, why not try another tack with her? Don't let nameless potential employers ruin what you two have got. For the kids and for your family — hell, even for the neighbors — why not try it? It sure beats having us for visitors, doesn't it?

Husband: Yeah, it sure would. *(Officer Clay reappears with woman)*

Officer Clay (to Officer Adams): I see you got him calmed down a bit. She, too, seems cooler. Her only complaint, really, is that he never talks to her. He just always comes home late and angry.

Officer Adams: Yeah, but maybe that will change. Let's take off. *(To couple)* Goodnight, now, and let's hope you can work it out. We don't like having to come over and I'm sure you don't either.

Husband: Thanks, we'll cool it.

Wife: Yeah, thanks.

Case 2: "The Nun"

Scene: *A young Catholic police officer has just stopped a nun for speeding. She has shown her driver's license and identification, which shows her to be a sister at a convent two counties away.*

Officer: I'm sorry to have had to stop you, sister, but my partner in the other car over there clocked you on radar 22 miles over the speed limit. I'm afraid I have no choice but to issue you a citation.

Sister: I'm sorry also, officer. I'm late right now for the Catholic Student Association meeting scheduled for this morning. I am the guest speaker there and I am very embarrassed by this.

Officer: With all due respect, sister, if there were any way I could forget about this, I would. But I can't. Are you going to be in town for long?

Sister: No, just for the day. My brother is one of the deans at the University and I'll be staying to have dinner with him.

Officer: Well, because you are from out of town, in fact out of the county, I normally would have to take you in and have you post bail for this ticket. You could also post your DL.

Sister: Oh, that would be terrible. I'd be late for my talk; in fact, I'm late now, and how embarrassing it would be to me and the dean.

Officer: Can I trust you, sister?

Sister: Of course you can. What do you mean by that?

Officer: Well, I'll tell you what I'll do. If you give me your word that you will either pay the fine through the mail or appear in court on the appointed date, which is October twenty-third, at 8:00 AM, I will let you proceed and not post a bond.

Sister *(Very coldly):* Well, THANK YOU, Officer. *(Fade out)*

Case 3: "The Sunglasses"

Scene: *Opens with an officer writing out a ticket to a young male subject. The camera looks over the shoulder of the officer and focuses on the face of the subject.*

Officer: Now you do understand, don't you, why I'm issuing you this citation? I followed your cycle for five blocks coming up University Drive here and at no time did your speed drop below 45 mph. The speed limit is 20 mph, as posted.

Subject: Yeah, but come on, officer. All students speed on this drive and I've never seen anyone get a ticket. How are you so sure I went 45 or better? Did you clock me with radar?

Officer: No, I *paced* you. That means that for five blocks I kept my patrol car the same distance from your cycle and at no time did your speed or mine drop below 45 mph.

Subject: Okay, big deal. Like I said, everyone does it. Why pick on me?

Officer: I'm not trying to pick on you. I simply happened to pick you up at a high rate of speed six or seven blocks down University Avenue. Take it easy. I'm only going to write you for a 38 in a 20 instead of a 45; that way you may get a break from your insurance company. *(Officer writes on ticket)*

Subject: You're getting a big kick out of this, aren't you? I can just see it! You're enjoying giving this college kid a hard time. You don't give a damn about me or any of us! Go to hell! Write it up for 45; I don't give a damn! *(Subject throws up his hands in anger, and officer looks back over his shoulder into the camera. Camera focuses on his reflecting, non-see-through mirror glasses.)*

The angry man will defeat himself
in battle as well as in life.
Samurai maxim

Fit voice to situation.
Author

VOICE 5
Creating a Character to Fit the Situation

THE crucial lesson to be learned from the last chapter is that no effective communication can take place without sensitive awareness of audience. Skillful audience analysis discovers the best available *means* to influence someone else. Once such means have been found, the next step is to fashion them in the appropriate VOICE. To know *who* one is speaking to is to know *how* to do it.

The last chapter ended with the assertion that *we make ourselves into what we have to become to relate effectively to the events, circumstances, personalities, and actions of others as we find them in the rhetorical situation.* The power that comes from the ability to adopt the appropriate voice and role to fit the present situation can be an officer's greatest asset in the streets. This chapter will examine the skills necessary to enable an officer to suit his voice and role to a situation.

WHAT IS VOICE?

By VOICE we mean verbal character. It is the dramatic persona or role that an officer adopts in the language he chooses. We all know, for example, that we do not speak to our parents the way we speak to our close friends. We speak with a different verbal character to our mother than to our father. Although we remain essentially the same person, we express our "self" differently to each. We use a different set of words, a different set of images, as we switch audiences.

Similarly, though an officer may say the same thing to his sergeant that he says to his partner, he will probably use different means. Suppose, for example, an officer had been criticized for his tactics during an arrest situation by his sergeant and by his partner. He might well disagree with both and defend his actions, but the words he uses to each will be quite different — or they had better be! The difference will lie partly in a change in TONE. Tone indicates the speaker's attitude towards the subject under discussion. Where the officer might be inclined to be sarcastic or condescending to his partner, he will not want to use that same tone with the sergeant for obvious reasons. Tone is part of the officer's total VOICE, but only a part. VOICE will be the sum of several elements, the most crucial being tone and level of voice modulation, any accompanying facial expressions (a sneer, for example), other hand or body gestures, and word choice (diction). If the officer is wise, he will change his verbal character (created by the above elements) as he switches from partner to sergeant. Like the chameleon, he will change surfaces as he confronts each.

VOICE AND ROLE: WHAT RELATIONSHIP?

Once an officer has clearly defined his audience, as a rhetorician he has to decide what ROLE to play to that audience. That role will be an IDENTITY created specifically for that audience and situation; in a way, the role will be a "mask," a face assumed to deal with the problems at hand. Because rhetoric is "situational," each rhetorical challenge will be different from the last and the identity assumed by the officer will vary with the changing scenes. Role playing is not falsification or insincerity; rather, it is a flexible way to deal with changing audiences and changing situations.

People role-play constantly. The officer who has had a fight with his wife before coming to work strives to be civil to his colleagues when he arrives for work. The officer who may have just left a class at the university, where he played the role of student, drops that role as he puts his uniform on; he becomes the street patrolman and his manner of carrying himself, his way of talking, possibly his entire demeanor, will change as he readies himself for police work. All of an officer's roles during a shift will be "dramatic" ones, for he will be acting in the theater of the streets. A role will be "good" or "bad" depending on whether it enables him to communicate with his audience and to effect his purpose.

VOICE is part of the total role adopted by the officer and it must be *consistent with* the assumed role. For example, if an officer wishes to assume the role of an understanding "father" to a fatherless juvenile delinquent, his voice should be in harmony with that intention. To be sarcastic or domineering would destroy the role before it ever had a chance to communicate with the juvenile. Similarly, if the officer wishes to act the role of impartial mediator between two parties, he must not allow his voice to come across as accusatory or biased. In this instance, an officer's PERSPECTIVE could interfere with his purpose and his chosen role would fail because of inconsistency.

ADOPTING ROLES: TECHNIQUES

To be able to create an appropriate role for a given situation returns us to the issues that we examined in the chapter on "Perspective" and to those in the chapter on "Audience." If an officer can control his own biases and if he can accurately analyze his audience, he should be able to fashion a suitable role to fit the occasion. Granted, some street officers will do this spontaneously, partly because they are actors at heart and partly because they are able to perceive the right responses almost automatically.

But all officers can learn to use certain techniques that will improve their chances of becoming who they must to handle situations. One such technique is the audience analysis step that we examined in the last chapter:

"Know the approximate relations to things as X knows them." The principle here is one of "similarity," not difference. There are only so many basic human emotions (e.g. rage, jealousy, greed, passion, love, hate, indifference), but the number of variations and mixtures is infinite. Although an officer's ability to *project* into the world of another can only be "approximate," this projection will enable an officer to better assess the communication options open to him given the nature of the subject he confronts.

How one projects into another's world, if only momentarily, is part mystery, part technique. To get an approximation of the relation to things as X knows them, however, one can use what I call the "spots of time" technique. Based on the assumption that we all have, at one time or another, experienced directly the basic human emotions that we encounter in police calls, the "spots of time" technique requires that we *recall* those moments as vividly as we can. Through such recall, we re-experience the emotions that we felt at the time. Because of the distance we have, however, we are not ruled by those emotions. The value of such recall is that we prepare ourselves to appreciate more fully the subject's present conflict. We begin to get a "sense" of what he must be going through at the time, making us more sensitive to the possible avenues of verbal persuasion.

Stanley L. Glenn (1977), in his book *The Complete Actor,* advises would-be actors:

> In dealing with the emotional behavior of a character in a play, true understanding is the result of the actor's ability to find parallels in his own experience. In order to do this, he must first abstract into universal terms the emotions portrayed. The actor may never have been confronted with the possibility of imminent death, but he has, in all probability, experienced the fears and anxieties of danger or of facing the unknown. His next step will be to find the specific incident in his own experience that may be related to the universalized emotion. When he succeeds in finding such an incident, he then proceeds to bring it alive through associations, in much the same way as he has done in reviving sensory responses. Out of his re-creation of as many of the details of the experience as possible, he concentrates upon the stimulus, the sensation, and the response, although his primary concern is in making the stimulus sufficiently vivid to cause sensation and response to become virtually automatic (p. 56).

I quote this passage at length because it defines several important steps an actor (or officer) should take to project. Finding parallels in one's own life to the basic emotion being portrayed is step one. Because of the limitless variations of human emotions, it is important that an officer abstract in universal terms the emotions (rage, jealousy, despair) he sees in his subject. Having done that, he can then recall an incident in his own life that aroused similar feelings and imaginatively relive the accompanying sensations and responses that were occasioned by it. In so doing, the officer mentally creates the "approximate" relation to things as X knows them. The "spots of time" technique, then, can help an officer build a bridge to the subject's way of seeing at the moment. He is then ready to take the next step.

Again we return to the "Audience" chapter and restate the principle that to know X effectively, the officer must *identify the role that X is playing out and stand in relation to that role.* Subjects who act out violent behavior usually do so because they have been frustrated by someone or some event in the external world. Some *expectation* has been frustrated, some role repudiated, and violence seems to offer some kind of revenge.

Whether the violent or disturbed subject is actually acting out a *role* can be difficult to tell, but it helps an officer relate to that subject if he can identify a "character" or role in the subject's actions. The avenger role is common, as is the role of scourge, master, even "cop." The man beating his wife may see himself as an "avenger," righting the wrong she has done to him, or as a "man," a "master," taking his rightful place as head of the family. The citizen who mixes into another person's family beef may see himself as the neighborhood "cop," dedicated to keeping people civil, or as the "savior" of one or more of the family members. Kurt Vonnegut, the writer, says in his novel, *Mother Night,* "We are what we pretend to be, so we must be careful about what we pretend to be." We all create roles for ourselves and then use our energy trying to play them successfully. When we succeed, we feel in harmony with "reality"; when we fail, we either modify or switch our roles so they better fit our being or we overreact and lash out at the world that doesn't seem to allow us to be who we think we can be.

It is the latter — those who lash out — that the street officer meets as a daily matter of course. If the officer can perceive the role of a subject, he can make an assessment of a proper counter-role that he might play to influence the subject. Since the officer will know "where the subject is coming from," he will be able to fit his own character to the situation as the subject sees it and thereby improve his chances of modifying or controlling him.

The officer's role is a "counter" role precisely because it must ultimately correct or modify the subject's — that is, it must work changes on the subject. But to counter successfully, the officer's role must in *some way* harmonize with the subject's perspective and role. If it does not, the relationship will be one of force against force. To *persuade* someone to do something that he doesn't wish to do takes strategy, and the strategy of the "counter-role" involves skillful positioning and selection of voice.

Consider the matter of *positioning:* the way in which you as officer stand in relation to the subject. If you stand squarely opposite him, you force confrontation; but if you stand obliquely to one side, off-center so to speak, you can deflect his force and use it to your own advantage. In judo, for example, the best way to throw someone is to move with his force, use his energy to your advantage. If your antagonist steps forward and pushes, you step to one side and move with his force, using it to make your own throw. The same philosophy holds true for the counter-role. The role you adopt should connect or align itself to the subject's direction and perspective (the initial harmony necessary) and then work on the subject in such a way as to move or "throw" him in the direction that you feel is necessary. The more you as officer relate to the role that the subject is playing out, the better your chances of influencing him. If you are handling a domestic dispute, for example, you will face at least two very different "stories" or "realities" concerning what happened: one from the wife, one from the husband. Presuming, as is the case much of the time in such calls, you have a partner with you, separate the two and have him take one to the side. As you face the other (the husband, for example), begin immediately to look for clues that will help you define the role he is playing out at the moment. In order for you to *position* yourself and adopt the appropriate role for the verbal encounter, you must, in the brief time allowed, make as many inferences as you can about the subject. If you take the time to listen to his side of the story and observe carefully the kind of language he uses to describe it, you should be able to ascertain with some accurary how he sees himself in the scene.

Without a doubt, language is one of the best indicators of personality; in a very real sense, we are how we speak. The images and examples that we use in describing an event, or a series of events, reveals our present preoccupations, our past experiences, and our concepts of ourselves. The husband who says to you that he "has taken all he can take and doesn't intend to lose another fight" reveals that he sees his domestic life in terms of an ongoing contest, a battle with winners and losers. He sees his marriage, in other words, as a prize fight in which the winner takes all — that's his image of it. As an officer, you know that relationships can be seen in more healthy terms, but if you intend to change the subject's abiding perspective, you must first work with it sympathetically. You might begin, for example, by *agreeing* that you, too, have lost your share of battles with the opposite sex; but you can *add* that your problem lay, you discovered, in habitually regarding discussions as battles to be won or lost. Once you changed that image, you saw that winning or losing was not the crucial issue. If the subject has children, you might lead him to see that winning over the wife might, in some way, be losing with the kids. Your goal, of course, is to leave the couple at peace, at harmony, and to do this you must *change* the "mental set" of each, change the way they see each other. The role you choose to adopt, in other words, has a dramatic purpose, and if the first role you try doesn't seem to work, drop it and try another. Where you are dealing with people who have become inflexible, you must remain loose and capable of rapid change of perspective and approach.

Your characterization or role, in short, is a *means* to an end, just as any emotion you show is a means to an end. Your character or *persona,* your "mask," must grow *out of the action of the present.* You do not want to enter any scene with a rigid or set "character." The initial positioning you do should involve "empathy" for the subject; that is, you behave *as if* you feel what the subject does, and by adopting an empathetic perspective towards the subject you will exhibit a pattern of behavior that creates the appropriate persona or mask for the occasion.

One reason why the Rogerian approach to communication that

we analyzed in the last chapter generally succeeds is that it stresses hearing the subject out, trying in two or three moves, to know the world as the subject sees it. It gives you time to position yourself and time to know as much as you can about the subject. When you don't have the luxury of time, close observation of the scene itself and close attention to the words you are able to hear are all you have to go on. In such cases, be prepared to change roles quickly as you see one that doesn't work efficiently.

Once you have decided on a rhetorical *position* with regard to your subject, your own *language* becomes crucial. Your voice, including the exact words you use (diction) and the tone you speak them in, must *harmonize* with your role. The subject that you are confronting has been responding to his own role, but when you enter the scene he begins as well to respond to your role. Everything you say or do makes a commitment and to which he will respond. By themselves, words make commitments. If you say, "Look here, Jack," the subject expects you to follow that with a declarative statement: "Do this or that." Moreover, if his name is not Jack, that word alone will, like a trigger of a revolver, spark an explosion.

If you, in the domestic dispute described above, have decided on a "participatory" approach — a "we-are-friends" approach — you must be very careful to word your questions and statements in that spirit. Since the subject feels abused, beaten, your questions should be worded in such a way that they show confidence in his ability to change the present situation. Questions like "Well, how would you like to see your wife change?", "What do you think would help the situation in the home?", or "Don't you think you should take the lead in straightening the problems out?" convey the sense that you are looking to the subject for direction, putting him in the position of strength in solving the problem rationally and non-violently. If the subject feels that you, the officer, has confidence in his ability to change the destructive nature of the home, he will more than likely wish, increasingly, to respond in that manner. Your expectations, created by the role that you have chosen and the language which mirrors it, can create in the subject, your audience, an approximate if not an identical expectation. True, initially you may believe that he is incapable of rational action, but if you adopt a role that exudes confidence that he will act with reason, often the subject will begin to respond to your expectations. The *illusion* of rationality becomes the *reality* of rationality primarily because you have made it happen. As we saw in the last chapter, you can *make* and *remake* your audience through the power of your controlling perspective and your adopted role.

But suppose your chosen role fails? Suppose, as you interact with the subject, you see that you are not moving him in the direction that you had hoped. What then? Clearly you must change your role, modify it, or throw it away and begin again. To do this effectively, you must make a *transition* from one role to the next, and the smoother the transition the better. Abrupt changes in direction may upset the subject more; you must effect a change without appearing to be phony or indifferent to his feelings.

Any change in role involves a change in either *position* or *voice*. You can change your position, from "friend" to "counselor," or from "advisor" to "instructor," for example, but whatever the change involves, you do not want to lose your "hold" on the subject. As in judo, you may switch the position of your hands or hip, but if you lose contact with your subject, you lose your advantage. In the domestic dispute mentioned, if you discover your role is not getting the subject to take some responsibility for the family beef, you might try shifting your role to that of the "public's voice;" that is, you begin to focus on how the neighbors feel about having to call the police because of his family's continuing violence. Here you might let the subject know that whether or not he wants to act rationally, he has little choice in the long run. If you have to return on another complaint, he'll find himself spending the night in jail.

Depending on who the subject is, this shift or adjustment of role to the "public's voice" will be more or less successful. If he is someone whom you have decided probably cares about his image in the community, who cares about his "reputation," the change in position will work. If, on the other hand, he clearly is someone who could care less about what others say, it won't work and you'll have to try another approach. Generally, you will know enough about the subject to make an accurate assessment of whether the public voice role would make a difference. The subject's neighborhood, home, and general "status" will give you clues.

With a change in position, then, a change in voice must follow.

The calm, rational, friendly voice, used with the first role, should gradually harden into the more abstract, depersonalized voice of the "public." In everything you say to the subject you try to express the *necessity* of considering others, perhaps suggesting probable consequences if he fails to do this. The trick or skill here partly lies in your ability to convey not your own personal view but that of the unnamed "others," his friends and neighbors. By so doing, you provide him with a new perspective, an outside view of his behavior as seen by others.

Assuming that you tried this ploy or shift with the subject, how do you keep "contact" with him without alienating him? You speak not for yourself but for those others, and you keep yourself out of that generalized category. You *act* as a mediator, a forecaster of possible problems, a warning voice. You will not be responsible for his troubles, others will be, and you'd hate to see that happen. So might go your dialogue. Your role conveys the attitude that you want to help, but if he continues to abuse his family, pressures will be such that you will have no choice but to act as the representative of others (which you are anyway). Your voice will reflect two meanings in this role: (1) you have his best interests at heart, and (2) you will finally be forced to move against him in the interests of public good.

In this extended example, I have stressed the importance of adjusting your role to the developing behavior of the subject in a gradual, smooth, almost unnoticeable manner. But there will be situations in which an *abrupt shift* might be more effective. Again, the entire rhetorical situation will guide you concerning which approach to take. For example, suppose in dealing with the above subject, you perceive that his family beefs result from his weak nature; he is easily cowed by others, including his wife. Should your "friendly" rational approach not work, you might decide to make a sudden shift to "command role" and dominate him by the simple force of your own personality. You make a sudden shift in your *voice,* replacing friendly persuasion with command: "You will cut this crap out, now. Any more problems here and you'll end up looking at bars." Your command presence controls and directs the scene.

There are advantages and disadvantages to such abrupt shifts in role and voice, and your decision will have to be based on the exigencies of the moment. The advantages in switching to command control in the scene above might be two: (1) you take control in a scene that has threatened to explode, and (2) *you* cow the subject, not the wife. If the subject has been accustomed to being dominated by his wife, with all its accompanying backlash, you, by your actions, change the situation, thus freeing her from blame. It is entirely possible that should you successfully browbeat the subject into compliance, his wife will take his side verbally and the two will come together with you as antagonist. When you leave, they will be in harmony.

The possible disadvantages, depending on the character of the subject, are these: first, he may allow himself to be controlled while you are on the scene, but as soon as you leave he will turn on the wife and take out his frustration on her. Most men will resent being overpowered or cowed by another man, especially in front of their wives or girl friends. You can diminish such backlash by making it as clear as you can to the subject that what you are doing is a professional necessity, not a personal win-lose battle. The more the subject sees your actions as those of a "public representative," the less likely he is to respond to you in a personal manner. Secondly, in driving the wife and subject together, against you, you run the risk of eventually having to fight two rather than one. But if you keep your voice free of personal satisfaction in your controlling of the subject, you are far less likely to antagonize the wife.

Whatever move you make, then, will entail rhetorical choices and rhetorical consequences. You must "read" the scene as well as you can, picking up nuances between the husband and wife as you go, and adjust your voice and position accordingly. In the hypothetical scene described, it will be important that you "keep contact" with both subjects, particularly with the husband. Even in your abrupt shift from "friend" to "control officer," you should so conduct yourself that the subject can never feel that you are "out to get him" or make him look bad. The more disinterested you can be, the better.

One crucial guideline to successful street rhetoric is that the *voice* should always harmonize with the *position* that you decide to take as you confront a subject. If you square off with a subject and confront him head-on, your voice must be commanding, precise, and confident. Any wavering in voice will suggest weakness and encourage the subject to resist. If, on the other hand, you decide to handle the subject obliquely (from the side), your voice must reflect your differing positions. For example, assume the left side to be the "liberal" approach side, the "friendly participatory" side, and the right side to be the more conservative, right vs. wrong, moralistic side. Your language and voice, when you approach from the left, will suggest closeness and understanding; repeated uses of the word "we" or "you and I" will be common. Your goal will be to bring the subject around because he wants you to approve of him. He wants to be friendly because you understand his problems and have been sensitive to them.

From the right side, however, your voice will shift with your change in position. Now you remind him of other people's rights, of what is clearly right or clearly wrong in the situation, and of his own responsibility to "clean up his act." Because your stress is on law, justice, and the rights of others (as well as his own rights), your voice will be more business-like, more formal, perhaps more teacher-like. You will be instructing and persuading, reminding and reasoning, and your voice must assume that tone of authority and knowledge.

The left and the right sides are really only metaphors for two basic approaches to resisting subjects; hundreds of variations are possible, of course, and only you, on the spot at the time, will know which one to try. But the metaphors of left, right, and head-on can help you remember the basic possibilities in approaches; your own imagination and intelligent audience analysis should do the rest in any given situation.

THE THREE BASIC MODES OF PERSUASION

The father of rhetoric, Aristotle, said that we persuade others by three means: (1) by the appeal to their *reason,* (2) by the appeal to their *emotions,* and (3) by the appeal of our *character* or *personality.* We may use one of these predominantly or we may use all three. Which approach we take will be determined by the rhetorical situation and its exigency (the problem), the set of constraints, and the audience. Our rhetorical perspective (PAVPO), particularly our *perspective* and our *purpose,* will also help us select the appeal(s). Whatever our approach, our *voice* and *position* must be consonant with it and be fitting for it.

Man's capability to reason distinguishes him from all other animals, but because he is an animal he too often forgets this essential trait and responds irrationally. Police officers, who represent man's reason as it finds expression in the law, often encounter people in this state and find themselves having to restore reason to its rightful place as commander of the senses and passions.

The appeal to reason has force, even with unreasonable subjects, because most people do not like to think of themselves as acting irrationally. Indeed, the "irrational" subject often believes himself quite "reasonable;" he, at any rate, sees "reason" for doing what he is doing, and it is up to the street officer to alter his perspective by showing, through argument or logic, that his position is not, in fact, reasonable, not at all what he thinks it to be. In order to accomplish this change in perception, the officer will have to listen carefully to the subject (as in the Rogerian approach to communication) and be capable of spotting logical problems with the subject's interpretation of the scene. The more training an officer has had in logical thinking and argument, the better his chances of persuading the subject, and the more calm and rational the officer *appears* while engaged in this task, the better his chances of success. The *voice* must reflect the calm, rational approach of the officer.

Whenever you as officer face an angry subject, listen carefully to the nature of his "argument." Although this chapter is not on logic, you need to know the four basic logical errors subjects are likely to make in talking with you, especially if you wish to use the appeal of reason in your counter-role. The first is what logicians call the EITHER/OR FALLACY, a tendency people have to see life in simple two-valued terms: black or white. The only time an either/or proposition will be valid is when the alternatives are exhaustive: "either he voted or he did not." Most human problems, however, are more complicated and involve more than two alternatives. Subjects who confront you with either/or statements, especially in states of anger, usually forget that there are other alternatives. Your job is to point out these other unseen alternatives and help them discover a third way. Most domestic disputes and street fights evolve because the situations became rigid, leaving only two alternatives. As police officer, you will often have to mediate between parties, and the way to do this is to show each party the other possible options.

A second common fallacy encountered on the street is the FAULTY GENERALIZATION or "hasty Gen." This occurs when people "jump to conclusions" based on inadequate evidence. Evidence can be faulty in a number of ways:

1. The particulars may be irrelevant.
2. The particulars may be unrepresentative.
3. The particulars may not be numerous enough to lead to the conclusions drawn from them. Moreover, often people will fight because of circumstantial evidence, things they have heard from others, but these, too, are liable to error.
4. The "evidence" can come from a biased source.
5. The evidence can come from an incompetent source.
6. Sources of information can also be inaccurately quoted, misunderstood, or quoted out of context. Whenever a subject tells you that he is reacting the way he is because of what he has learned from someone else, remember the possible problems in sources mentioned above and move the subject towards thinking about the sources themselves. This may deflect his anger for a moment and bring him to a more reasonable position.

A third common fallacy in argument is the FAULTY CASUAL GENERALIZATION, and this comes about whenever subjects assign an inadequate cause to an effect or when they fail to consider the possibility of multiple causes. The subject who concludes that his wife is cheating on him because she has come home late from work three nights in a row commits such a blunder. She may have been late for any number of reasons, but the subject has jumped from *effect* (she comes home late) to *cause* (she is seeing someone else) without considering other possible causes. Listen carefully to your subject's "story" to spot hasty generalizations or faulty-cause arguments; once you spot such probable fallacies, adopt a calm and reasonable voice to fit your appeal to reason and attempt to make the subject THINK about what he has been saying. In this manner you have shifted the subject's attention from conclusions to means of reasoning, and such a shift often causes a change in dominant perspective and mood.

The fourth major fallacy, common to most street problems, is the

AD HOMINEM argument, or the argument "against the man." You see this fallacy whenever you hear a subject switch from the issues under debate to a discussion of personalities. A man's character has some relevancy when the issue being argued has to do with reliable testimony or the likelihood of his having done something, but even in such instances more evidence than a man's character is necessary to make valid inferences. When a subject tells you "X must have done it (some event) because he is that kind of asshole," you have a clear example of an ad hominem argument. So, too, in the comment, "Well, you know the type; she's a divorcee." The more you can center a subject's attention on evidence — facts, data, details — the less likely he is to react personally. To ask, "What are the facts here?" generally forces people to take a different stand than the ad hominem approach, thus increasing the chances of a rational discussion.

In all appeals to *reason,* an officer must assume the role of inquisitor. He must listen carefully and then question what he hears in an effort to make the subject do the same. The nature of the dialogue between subject and officer will be one of inquiry rather than reaction. As the officer investigates the nature of the call, he gets the subject to assume a similar stance. When inquiry replaces emotion, reason regains its rightful place as arbiter and the problem has a good chance of being solved in a peaceful manner.

For the officer, the appeal to the *emotions* can be effective if handled indirectly. If a subject is aware of the fact that you intend to play on his emotions to get him to do something, he will resist you. The emotional appeal is probably the strongest appeal; all people are affected by the emotion of others. Police calls generally come as a result of emotional collisions among people, and the challenge of the job is to shift the emotional levels between people as much as possible.

In the emotional appeal your chosen role is crucial, for you cannot convey emotion unless you first "feel it" yourself. The "spots of time" technique mentioned earlier helps you create the appropriate kind of empathy for the subject's emotional state, thus preparing you to relate effectively to the subject. Whenever you wish to displace a negative emotion and replace it with a healthier one, you must yourself "express" that emotional state. One way to do this is to use the kind of words that will embody the emotion you wish to raise in the subject. Words carry an emotional force far beyond their literal meanings and this force is called CONNOTATION.

Connotation: The Hidden Force of Words

Words convey two kinds of meaning: literal and figurative, denotive and connotative. The denotive meaning of a word is its dictionary meaning, its literal definition. But most words carry a second kind of meaning, an emotional meaning. Connotation is the emotional charge or resonance of a word and it always involves association. That is, because a word becomes associated with certain feelings and memories, it carries additional force, a force that can trigger powerful reactions. Consider how you would feel if someone called you a "socialist." The literal meaning of the word refers to a system or condition of society in which the means of production are owned and controlled by the state. But the word would, to most Americans, carry very negative associations; it would be associated with communism, totalitarianism, and subversive behavior despite the fact that England and Sweden are socialistic countries. Were you a Russian, of course, you would respond favorably to the word "socialist" and negatively to a word like "democracy."

In learning to use words to create a voice capable of moving an audience, you must carefully consider the connotative values of the words that you employ. Generally, connotation draws from four basic sources: appeals to the senses, to beliefs, to prejudice, and to insecurity. Being conscious of these sources, and understanding them fully, can help you control the emotional levels of your own voice and direct those levels in others.

Appeals to the Senses

Since connotation functions essentially by association, many words become charged because of their sensory appeal. Words like "crisp" and "crackling" may help to sell lettuce or cereal, but words like "slippery" or "stingy" may, when applied to someone's character, retard or destroy any possible communication. In each set of instances, the positive or negative feelings associated with the words come from our sensory memory banks. To "sell" a point of view to a subject, an officer must choose only those words that will trigger positive reactions. Should he wish the subject to leave a tavern, for example, he might advise him to "slide on outta here" and the subject might think that would be a neat thing. But if the officer used the word "sneak," the subject might well resist because he associated the word with a guilty child's behavior, an image he would fight. Where the word "slide" would suggest a skillful movement (as in baseball or basketball — to slide by a defender), "sneak" would conjure up images of cringing to avoid contact. Moreover, aside from the sensory impression of cringing, the word also would conjure up images contrary to the subject's set of beliefs, another source of connotation.

Appeals to Beliefs

All persons have particular attitudes and beliefs, and many of our everyday words refer to traditional values such as honesty, self-reliance, fair play, loyalty, courage, and "manly" conduct. Whenever an officer speaks to someone in the performance of his duty, he must be careful not to insult that person's value system. In the case of the subject in the tavern, to tell him to "sneak" out the back door suggests that he is a coward. Even if the officer means well (he just wants to get the subject out of harm's way), the subject will resist because of the connotation of the word "sneak."

Police officers often work in neighborhoods quite *unlike* their own (racial or ethnic communities, for example) and one real danger is that they will be indifferent, ignorant, or hostile to the prevailing attitudes and values of the community. Many, therefore, will unwittingly use language that irritates or antagonizes. To insist, for instance, that one Hispanic apologize to another will likely lead to trouble, for there is no word for "apologize" in Spanish. It is a foreign concept. Likewise, to talk about "compromise" — a good thing for most Anglo-Saxons — will bring only more problems because such an idea is abhorrent to Spanish peoples. The closest word for it is *"compromiso,"* which means a date.

If an officer is working a Hispanic-American community, he should know that Hispanics tend to value *being* over *doing,* a distinction that makes an argument based on *individualism* and *personalism* strong and one based on *productivity* and *efficiency* weak. So, too, the Spanish concept of *mañana* illustrates not laziness but concentration on the present rather than the future. In trying to appeal to Hispanics in a disturbance call, for example, an officer will have greater rhetorical force if he uses words that relate, literally and connotatively, to present concerns and not future ones.

The more an officer knows about the culture of the people with whom he deals, the better his chances of influencing them without unknowingly irritating or insulting them. He will be more capable of using words with positive connotations. Emotional response to language is natural and inescapable; the shrewd street officer will choose his language intentionally given the particular nature of his audience. In this way he will not precipitate additional problems because he has been unaware or insensitive to other people's attitudes and beliefs.

Appeals to Prejudice

A more complex form of connotation reminds us of our stereotypes and biases, images that we all carry around with us that refer to racial types, ethnic origins, professions, organizations, political affiliations . . . the list is endless. For the street cop, racial connotations can be the most dangerous because they readily trigger violent responses. Using loaded words like "nigger," "wop," "kike," "spic," or "honkey" practically guarantees trouble. One goal of communication is to bring the "outsider" *inside,* to make a bridge across which understanding can travel from one person to another. Employing racially loaded words, for example, shuts down avenues of communication. For a white cop to tell a black driver that if he doesn't want trouble with the police he's "gonna have to learn to drive like a white man in this here town" sets the stage for violence or for a letter of complaint to the chief. Likewise, negative references to women (male chauvinism in action) will produce trouble on the scene and later through departmental channels. Unless you have a good reason, you don't want to call a woman a "girl" or a "babe," nor make such chauvinistic distinctions as those between "man's work" and "woman's work."

Appeals to Insecurity

Another source of connotation is the area of insecurity and personal needs. All people crave approval, desire to be thought successful, intelligent, or sexually attractive. Few wish to be thought timid, fearful, or dull. People desire status, whether financial or otherwise, and these hopes and desires can usually be seen in the roles people play out daily. The sensitive officer will sense a subject's areas of insecurity and, if he wishes to calm or reassure him, he will use words that point towards strength. Should he, however, wish to break the subject down, he will choose words that play strongly on the subject's anxieties and fears.

Again, audience analysis becomes important. One man's area of insecurity is another man's area of strength. You must observe your subject carefully, listen to him intently, and then draw what inferences you can about his verbal world. Your selection or diction (word choice) will be based on this analysis. Because you have to persuade or manipulate people daily, you must be sensitive to your language in action. The use of connotation, or slanted language, can be very useful on the street in a rhetorical situation. Obviously, such slanted language does not belong in your report on the incident later. Here, because your audience has changed (it is now the department and "public record"), you should empty your sentences of all loaded words and be as objective as possible in detailing what actually happened.

Depending on the unique situations, you will choose to make an appeal to *reason* or to *emotion;* in many cases you will attempt to combine the two approaches, using emotion in your appeal to reason, and vice versa. The third basic means of appeal is called the *ethical appeal* and this refers to the persuasive force of your character or "persona." Aristotle argued that one's own speech or words can impress an audience that the speaker is a man of sound sense, high moral character, and benevolence. Notice that it is what you say that produces this impression. Your entire discourse must create and maintain the "image" that you seek to establish. We are back to the familiar concept that you must *make* yourself what you believe you must be to handle a situation. Your selection of *voice* will be crucial here, for as soon as you begin to speak you begin to make your ethical appeal.

The most important moments in any verbal exchange occur in the beginning and at the end. You set the tone of the ensuing discourse as soon as you enter a room or confront a subject in the street. You set before the subject your "character," your presence, and, even if you find you have to shift voices and roles repeatedly throughout the scene, your ethical appeal must be persuasive throughout. Any lapse from good sense, good will, or moral integrity can destroy your appeal. A note of ill will or personal distaste, a flash of illogic or inaccuracy, or any obvious bias or prejudice can ruin your persuasive effort. In other words, setting and maintaining your basic ethical character can be crucial to your success as a persuader.

Before you leave the scene you will want to reinforce your ethical appeal, making an explicit attempt to maintain your credit and good will with your audience. Part of your continuing ethical appeal will be your reputation as a street officer (your street reputation), and no matter what the outcome of the particular situation might be, if you can leave your audience with the sense that you have been openminded, fair, and good willed, as well as tough enough to have done what needed doing, your force as a representative of law and order will be significantly enhanced. The "proper image" you want consistently to perpetuate is that of the "good man speaking;" this image can be your most potent force.

In selecting a role and a voice to match, you can draw from the three appeals of *reason, emotion,* and that of your own "character." Throughout this chapter, the emphasis has been on fitting your voice and rhetorical position to the situation that you face. Although you may be forced to adopt several voices and positions during any one encounter and use reason or emotion alternately, underneath it all you will want to sustain a dominant ethical image. Your authority and command presence depend far more on this underlying image than on the physical presence of your badge. Indeed, your badge is only a symbol of what you must create and re-create daily in the presence of others through your own persuasive powers.

MINI-CASES ON VOICE

General Directions

Read each case twice to become familiar with the details, determine if the cases are successes or failures, and then take the following steps:

1. Determine the EXIGENCY in each case.
2. List as precisely as you can the SET OF CONSTRAINTS present in the scene.
3. Analyze the AUDIENCE in each. List characteristics and note whether the officer or case worker is sensitive to these during the scene.
4. Describe the officer's PERSPECTIVE in the opening. Are biases reflected in the way he/she performs his/her duty?
5. Examine the VOICE employed by the officer or case worker. Is it appropriate to the situation? Does it shift during the scene, appropriately or inappropriately? Are "trigger" words used? Which ones? What *roles* are adopted? Successful?
6. Does the officer or case worker seem clear of purpose?
7. Pinpoint where the officer or case worker begins to have trouble, if at all. What mistakes, if any, are crucial and which ones concern which rhetorical elements of PAVPO?
8. Consider alternative ways to have handled the problem. Consider alternative roles and voices. Which might have served better in each particular instance?

Case 1: "JD"

Scene: *JD is a 15-year-old boy who has been arrested numerous times for shoplifting. In this latest instance, a social worker, Ms. K, comes to the home to talk with the parents and with JD. The court has recommended that social services look into the home environment of JD before it passes sentence on him. In this slice of scene, the parents and the boy are standing in the living room listening to Ms. K.*

Ms. K.: Now, folks, as you know, my job is to talk to all three of you in order to attempt to assess the possible causes of JD's continuing problem with shoplifting. It's often in the home, you know.

Father: Hey, there ain't no problem here, lady, except maybe having you come in here like a god telling us our roles. We know what we're doing.

Ms. K.: Oh, really? It seems from the rash of arrests that JD has had that something must be wrong somewhere and, as we know in psychology, the home is usually the best place to look. From your point of view, I gather you don't think there is a problem.

Father: "AS WE KNOW FROM PSYCHOLOGY . . ." — Jesus, that's what I really need here. I didn't say there wasn't a problem, lady, I just don't like you coming in and telling us we're at fault. We've done everything we can for JD here, but he just don't want to listen. He wears headphones all the time and mopes around giving me dirty looks — his Mom, too.

Ms. K.: And just what have you done to help JD through this stage? It is a stage, you know. All kids get uncommunicative at about his age.

Father: Yeah, all perfectly natural, right? I figured you'd say that! Well, I'll tell you what I do. Every time he steals, I take something he values away from him. He lost his headphones last time; this time it may be his bed!

JD: BIG DEAL! He calls himself a father, what a laugh! He enjoys dumping on me. I never do right; it's always, "Why don't you do like Bobby or Sammy do?" He never likes me for me! He always has someone "better" in mind and I'm supposed to be that!

Ms. K.: You know, JD's got a point there. Do you really feel that the way to cure him of stealing is to take more from him? Do you feel that constantly comparing him to others is going to give him a good self-image?

Father: I don't give damn about his self-image! He's got to get it into his head that he isn't at the center of the universe. Why I'm saddled with him I don't know, but he sure does make my nights a nightmare!

JD: Hey, yeah, why don't you listen to her? You think you know everything, don't you? You won't listen just because she's a woman. I know you, you don't listen to anyone!

Mother: Oh, stop it, all of you! I listen to this all the time. Fight, fight, fight! *(On verge of tears and shaking her fists)* These two go at it all the time. I don't know what to do!

Ms. K.: At least, ma'am, you admit there's a problem. He, there, doesn't see any. *(Gestures at husband)* Why don't you and I and JD, here, go into another room and have a chat about things?

Father: Hey, I'll tell you what you can do — GET OUT! You ain't chatting with anyone here. We can take care of our own problems! We don't need you splitting us more!

Mother: Oh, please leave. This is just getting worse and worse. He'll go slamming out of here in a minute, as usual, and JD will either duck out the back door or close himself off in his room. Please, just go!

Ms. K.: But you do realize, don't you, that the court ordered me to make an investigation, and much of JD's future may rest on what we do or don't do here today. You'll talk to me, won't you, JD?

JD: Hell, no. If you can't relate to my parents, what makes you think you can relate to me? That is your BIG word, isn't it? RELATE?

Ms. K.: Maybe we could do just that if we could just get your dad to step aside for a few moments.

JD: Why should he? It's his house — that's what he's always telling me, and I somehow don't think you're going to do us very much good.

Scene: *Camera fades with social worker shaking her head and turning to leave.*

Case 2: "Officer Keel"

Scene: *Officer Keel and his partner have been called to a residence concerning an impending assault. The officers know the following information. The neighborhood is a racially mixed one, low income, with frequent problems in neighbor relations. In this case, one sub-*

ject is reported to be threatening another subject with a baseball bat. As the officers arrive, they see a large crowd standing in the yard of the residence, surrounding two subjects, one of whom holds the baseball bat. He looks ready to swing at the other subject.

Officer Keel *(Getting out of his vehicle and approaching the crowd):* All right! That's enough of that! Back off, everyone. BACK OFF! NOW!

Scene: *The crowd turns towards the approaching officers. The subject with the bat lowers it slightly. The other subject says nothing.*

Officer Keel *(Pointing to the subject with the bat):* You, there, put that thing down, NOW!

Subject 1 *(with bat):* Hell, no! This son of a bitch beat up my sister because she wouldn't walk with him in the park. He beat the hell out of her and I'm gonna take it out of his ass! *(Several voices in the crowd yell, "Yeah, we saw it too! He did it and he's got it coming to him!")*

Officer Keel: I'm tired of telling you people to get along! If you can't act like normal people, then you deserve to be locked up. All of you! Now, everyone beat it, and you there, give me that bat! If you don't, I'll take it away from you. And you *(to the crowd),* stay out of it or I'll arrest you all!

ANALYSIS: Along with answering the basic questions, think about these:

1. What, most likely, will be the response from the crowd and from the subject with the bat?
2. Examine Officer Keel's word choice, his diction. What words does he use that are particularly loaded and dangerous given the described situation?
3. What mistakes in *audience analysis* does he make?
4. By his language, what "truths" about human behavior does he ignore? In other words, about what issues is he dangerously insensitive?
5. What role is the subject with the bat playing out? Does Officer Keel respond to this in any way?
6. What counter-role does Officer Keel adopt? Is it appropriate?

Case 3: "Officer Tuckness"

Scene: *The scene is the same residence as in the last case. Same call. A large crowd, a subject with a baseball bat, and an apparent "victim," the subject accused of beating up the sister of Subject 1. Officer Tuckness, with partner, arrives at the scene. He notices that the crowd is agitated and that Subject 1 is preparing to swing on Subject 2. As he gets out of his patrol vehicle, he pulls his nightstick.*

Officer Tuckness *(As he walks towards the crowd and the two subjects, he bangs his nightstick on several of the street lamp poles in his path):* All right, that's enough of that! You with the bat, BACK OFF! *(He punctuates his directions with a loud smack of the stick against a tree trunk in the front yard.)* The crowd draws back and the two subjects back away from each other a few paces.

Subject 1: Hey, look here, officer, this guy beat my sister because she wouldn't walk with him in the park. He marked her real good and I'm gonna do the same to him. He's got it coming! *(Shakes the bat at Subject 2)*

Crowd: *(Several voices):* Yeah, we saw part of it, right down the block there. He slapped her upside the head twice. He's got it coming.

Officer Tuckness *(Looking around at the crowd, searching for several known faces from the neighborhood):* Okay, okay, settle down a bit. I can't help if I don't know the score. Gimme some time. *(He beckons to two people he has dealt with successfully before.)* Can you two give my partner a hand? I'll need to talk to Subject 2 in a moment, but I want him to stay where he is and you can help. Okay? *(The two called forward walk towards Officer Tuckness' partner and join him around Subject 2. Officer Tuckness walks over to Subject 1 who still has the bat in his right hand.)*

Officer Tuckness: Look, before you get yourself in real trouble over something that you may be right about, let's have a chat and see if we can work out a better solution than going to jail for assault.

Subject 1: Look, officer, in this neighborhood we learn to take care of our own problems. If I let him get away with what he did to my sister, I'll be laughed out of here. It's a matter of pride, man, that's all. *(Pointing to an older adult figure)* Even my dad will tell you that. He's not too happy about what happened to Maggie, either.

Officer Tuckness *(Beckoning to the person described as the father):* Sir, would you join me over here? We need to do some talking. *(To Subject 1)* What's your name, sir?

Subject 1: Bobby D'Angelo. And in my family we don't take shit off anyone. Isn't that right, dad?

Father: That's right, officer. We don't, and that scum's gonna get his.

Officer Tuckness: Look, if what you say is true, and I'll investigate, you can be sure he'll get what's coming to him. But there are ways and there are ways to get the job done. The way you do it can make all the difference. *(To father)* Do you want Bobby to go to jail? Get a bad record? Lose money — all at the same time? *(To Bobby)* How about you? How much is doing it your way worth?

Bobby: To crush his head is worth it all. I ain't gonna take his kind of crap.

Officer Tuckness: I can understand that, all right; but suppose I could show you another, better way, a way that would wind up causing the subject more trouble in the long run? What then?

Bobby: Shit, you guys can't do much. You leave and he'll still be here.

Father: Wait, son, let's hear him out.

Officer Tuckness: Look, I can understand the matter of saving face, especially before this crowd, and the crowd is with you. It, too, thinks the subject has it coming. Note that there are witnesses to his attack. Let me get the facts. If what you and they say is true, I can take the subject to jail. He'll lose face in front of the crowd, lose time and money, and earn a police record all at the same time. That's what I call PUNISHMENT for an act. If you go your way, I'll have to call reinforcements, we'll battle in the streets, and eventually you, your dad, and your friends will go to the same place he will: to jail. Revenge, especially for a real wrong, is never sweet if you have to suffer along with the doer. Think about it. In this case, the easy way is the most punishing.

Father *(To Officer Tuckness)*: Can I have a moment to talk to my son?

Officer Tuckness: Sure. I'll step over here and see what my partner's got.

Father: This Tuckness guy is all right; I've heard he's fair and tough. We can't afford to battle the cops and then pay them at the jail house. Let's give him a chance to put this guy away. If he doesn't come through this time, we'll do it our way anyway, without witnesses.

Bobby: Okay, I'll try it. But if Tuckness doesn't come through and the guy gets off, I'll take care of it my way. Agreed?

Father: Yep. *(To Officer Tuckness)* Do it your way. We've got witnesses and we'll use them. What did ya find out over there?

Officer Tuckness: We've got enough to go on; we've got statements from three people; and if your sister will talk to me, we shouldn't have any problem. My partner is placing the subject under arrest now.

ANALYSIS: Along with answering the basic questions posed earlier at the beginning of these cases, think about the following:

1. In handling a crowd situation, Officer Tuckness employs several techniques. Define his strategies.
2. What *knowns* does Officer Tuckness use to help him work through the *unknowns* of the situation?
3. What APPEALS TO REASON does Officer Tuckness use?
4. What APPEALS TO EMOTION?
5. What ETHICAL or personality APPEALS does he use?

Softness triumphs over hardness,
feebleness over strength.
What is more malleable is always superior
over that which is immoveable.
This is the principle of controlling things
by going along with them,
Of mastery through adaptation.
Lao-Tzu

PURPOSE AND ORGANIZATION
Moving an Audience and
Shaping a Street Encounter
6

CLARITY OF PURPOSE

I HAVE chosen to combine the two rhetorical elements of PURPOSE and ORGANIZATION in one chapter because in street work the two are inseparable. Only when you are sure of your PURPOSE can you make skillful decisions about how best to ORGANIZE or shape your verbal encounter. In other words, STRUCTURE is discovered in PURPOSE.

PURPOSE is the heart of good police work; you are known by *what* you do and *how* you do it. Whenever you are called to a scene, you are called for a reason; one of the essential skills you must develop is the ability to discover and sustain a clear sense of purpose throughout a street encounter. To lose sight of your purpose is to generate new problems for yourself and others. As you saw in the earlier chapters, the rhetorical situation is a complex one, involving an exigency or central problem, an audience, a set of constraints, and your own presence as officer. Any one of these elements can become the source of trouble if you allow yourself to become fuzzy or unsure of your purpose.

For example, if you have been asked by a tavern proprietor to remove two abusive and disorderly subjects, you must do it quickly and efficiently. However, in such a scene you are likely to be surrounded by numerous subjects who are also loud and obnoxious and if you do not adhere strictly to your purpose, you can easily become derailed by such typical side-commentary as "HEY, PIG!" or "HERE COME THE STORM TROOPERS!"

The two major constraints in such a scene are (1) the sheer numbers of people in the area and (2) the confined nature of the tavern itself. To work successfully, you must accomplish your purpose of removing the two subjects without also involving those in the crowd; in other words, you must limit your audience to the two subjects and the proprietor. To enlarge your audience by including those vocal patrons is unwittingly to create an unnecessary purpose — saving your own skin.

Unfortunately, in the majority of police calls, purpose is not as clear as in our example. Calls that request you "See the man at . . . " or "Investigate the disturbance at . . . " are generally calls that will force you to define the appropriate purpose given your assessment of the facts you discover, the laws involved with those facts, and the total rhetorical situation. In such cases, it is helpful to have some basic guidelines to aid you in the search for appropriate purpose.

DETERMINING PURPOSE

Purposes fall into two classes: non-persuasive and persuasive. In the first instance, the primary goal is to inform or clarify; in the second, to alter radically or to reconstruct a person's ideas.

As officer, you will find yourself doing both each day you work on the streets; you will also be asked repeatedly to apply your knowledge of the law in non-persuasive and persuasive situations. One mark of your professionalism will be your grasp of the legal codes and another your ability to apply them in the given situation. Know the law as well as you possibly can, for to appear on a scene with an inadequate understanding of the legal codes is to be *unarmed* in a most dangerous way. Your ignorance will make you unsure of purpose, hesitant in performance, and a weak negotiator in stress situations.

In any scene, to determine purpose you must ascertain the *facts* at issue and assess the total *rhetorical complexities* present in the situation. Three basic approaches can help you accomplish this task skillfully: (1) assume the role of *questioner,* (2) be the source of crucial declarative *statements,* and (3) be an intense *listener.*

Playing the role of questioner is fundamentally important because you can control a scene by asking certain kinds of questions in specific ways. Indeed, it is through questioning that you discover the needs of your audience and, often, determine your central purpose. The number of questions you can ask is infinite, but the kinds of questions you employ in your investigation are finite. Most questions fall into one of five categories:

1. *The fact-finding question:* "Who," "What," "Where," "When," "Why," and "How." These are the journalist-like questions that we examined in Chapter 2.
2. *The general question:* "What do you think?" "Why did she do it?" "Why did you do it?" "What really went on here?" Because these questions pose no limit, they are not controllable; that is, the answers you get can go anywhere or lead to anything, so you must be ready to handle possible trouble triggered by the answers.
3. *The direct question:* "Who can solve this problem?" "Who else is involved?" Because the questions are direct, they contain some limits and therefore the answers can be controllable.
4. *The leading question:* "Isn't this true?" "Isn't it a fact that. . . .?" The leading nature of such questions makes the answers controllable.
5. *The opinion-seeking question:* "Do you think?" "Is it?" "What does your wife think?" "What do your neighbors think?" The answers are controllable if you keep your questions tailored to the kinds of information that you want to elicit.

Although these categories are not always clearly different, for occasionally there will be overlapping questions, basically they represent the five kinds of questions that you can use to develop information and a sense of your audience's needs and desires. To know that questions themselves serve different purposes is the first step in learning to act with judgment and discretion in the midst of an emotionally stressful scene. As the "outsider" in most disputes and controversies, you must consider carefully the kind of questions you want to ask and the way in which you want to structure those questions. Questions control the kind and the amount of information that you receive and the direction that the verbal exchange takes while you are on the scene. In scenes that call for the presence of an officer, conclusions and judgments probably are dominant in the minds of the participants. As you enter the scene, you can bring a new tenor and perspective to it by interjecting a battery of carefully designed questions to make the participants *think* more critically and disinterestedly about the issue under consideration. Good questions provoke thoughtful responses; bad questions, or ill-timed questions, precipitate additional problems or bring a halt to all fruitful discussion.

In any problematic situation, you are best served by asking the *fact-finding* questions first. By so doing, you acquaint yourself with the basic facts of the situation, but you may also learn a good deal about your audience if you listen carefully to the answers to your questions. The areas of controversy should become apparent as your witnesses respond to the fact-finding questions. Providing a space of time in which facts can be gathered gives time for the disputants to calm down; your authority gives you the power to ask these questions, and by asking them you force the people involved to *reconstruct* the situation as they see it — according to "the facts." A good rule of thumb during this initial period of questioning is to disallow all statements not directly related to fact finding. Inform the participants that you will give them time later to give their opinions and judgments. In so doing, you prevent emotional discharges of all sorts and yet you also let it be known that you value personal judgments enough to hear them at a later time.

Depending on what answers you get by asking the fact-finding questions, make your decision regarding what other kinds of questions to ask and in what order. As a guideline, it is best to prepare some groundwork before asking the general, the direct, the leading, or the opinion-seeking questions, especially in situations of high emotional tension. Whenever possible, explain *why* you intend to ask a certain question. By giving your reasons for asking a personal question, for example, you prepare the subject for the kind of question that will follow and you create the impression that you are sensitive to that person's feelings. As an "outsider," you are likely to embarrass or anger a subject without intending to do so because of your ignorance of the total situation, so the more preparation you can give to each of your questions the better.

Unless you are trying to trap a subject into revealing information that he otherwise might not give, you are generally more successful in your questioning if you provide the subject with an overview of the kind of information that you must eventually have to make a good decision. Subjects tend to react more positively to a battery of questions if they have the general plan of inquiry from the outset. Such an overview also lessens the chance that the information they give you will be irrelevant; in other words, providing an overview makes your whole process of questioning more efficient.

For any sequence of questions, your own persona or character will be a crucial ingredient. Unless your purpose is to intimidate a subject, try not to ask questions that, in their very wording, convey any personal biases that you have toward the subject. Your job is not to humiliate the subject but to elicit information as concisely and fully as you can. Above all, be careful that the role you adopt does not actually interfere with your central purpose of getting the necessary information. To adopt, for example, a superior tone with a street subject is not only likely to increase the subject's dislike of you but will also yield little information. Likewise, questions that carry vague, negative implications about the subject, his family, or his behavior will develop very little useful information. In getting information, like so much else in police work, *you must become what you have to* in order to accomplish your purpose.

Particularly useful for creating and sustaining good will during questioning are the general questions and the opinion-seeking questions, for both appear to value the subject's view of the situation. Once you have ascertained the basic facts of a case, these two types of questions allow subjects to provide their own points of view, to vent their personal feelings, and to offer suggestions for solving the problem at hand. The fact-finding questions have provided the necessary cooling-off period. The general and opinion questions should now have a more reasonable chance of extracting or evoking useful information and suggestions for resolution of the problem.

Moreover, the general question and the opinion-seeking question are both useful inquiry tools to help you uncover those hidden assumptions and biases that so often are the causes of violent behavior. To make a good street decision, you must not only know *what* happened and *to whom* but also *why* it happened. Once you know the causes of a problem, you have a much clearer sense of what laws, if any, are involved and what persons, if any, are responsible. As a mediator, one who tries to create a climate of negotiation in the midst of conflict, you must attempt to probe subjects for those hidden assumptions, which may also often not be fully understood by the subjects themselves. Once you have uncovered such, you can focus your direct and leading questions directly on the substance of these assumptions.

A well-known negotiating strategy allows participants to present their various sides of an issue until real conflict in point of view becomes clear. At this point, the negotiator stops all further discussion and insists that the opposing parties, one by one, restate their positions as clearly and as objectively as possible. During the restatement period, the other parties must not interrupt or disagree. The value of this "restatement" strategy is that it encourages listening and critical thinking while taking away the opportunity to react emotionally.

Think how useful such a strategy might be for a domestic dispute in which the parties involved had reached a verbal impasse. At that point — a point marked by real conflict of interpretation — you as officer would institute the "restatement of position" device. The husband would have uninterrupted time to restate his entire position while the wife listened and then she would have a similar period of time. At the completion of this restatement time, each party then has the opportunity to question the other regarding any matters of CLARITY. Such questions as "Did you mean this by that?", "How exactly do you define your view of 'reasonable'?", or "What do you mean by the word 'X'?" delay the impulse to disagree and encourage the impulse to understand. As such, then, they serve as important psychological devices as well as information-getting devices.

At times, depending on the situation, the above procedure will bring sufficient harmony to the scene to make further police work unnecessary. At other times, however, it will only begin to make a significant difference. Under such conditions, you can institute a second strategy of asking the warring parties to state as clearly as they can the precise position of their antagonists. In the case of the domestic dispute, this strategy would ask the husband to restate his wife's position as neutrally as humanly possible, then the wife would have to do the same. Like the first strategy, this one — essentially the Rogerian method we examined in the chapter on audience — encourages reflective, problem-solving stances. Because you have insisted that the participants remove the adversary nature of their approach to the problem (for at least a temporary time), you have created a climate in which the participants have a better than even chance of actually *hearing* and *understanding* one another. In such a climate, they have a good opportunity to discover the real, as opposed to the apparent, sources of conflict and thus begin to move towards a suitable resolution.

Such strategies as the "restatement" strategy and the Rogerian strategy are valuable both for the disputants and for you. The subjects get some "breathing room" and a chance to be heard; you get an abundance of information that you might not get in any other manner, and you have additional time to make the kind of psychological assessments you must if you hope to adopt an appropriate role that can help you interact effectively with the subjects. By your authority you have created a learning environment in the midst of conflict and have thus shifted the dominant stress of the scene from frozen disputed positions to more open, flexible, problem-solving positions.

But as you attempt to make this shift in a scene, you have other possible options other than the role of *questioner;* you may also be the central source of *statements,* particularly at those moments where you see you have unearthed a dominant bias or assumption in one of the subjects that may be the basis of his or her violent reactions. Rather than contradict the bias or assumption, thus precipitating more possible violence, you usually have more success if you make an affirmative statement such as "I know how you feel" or "I've often felt that way, too." Although you eventually hope to move the subject from that bias or negative underlying assumption, you first show understanding of it, thus lessening his or her defiance and creating an atmosphere of continuing discussion.

At the same time that you state that the subject's bias is understood, you will also want to indicate that it needs additional thought or analysis; if you make some initial *concession* to the subject (in this case, his view has some validity or substance), then you have a better opportunity to move him to consider possible weaknesses in his bias and which may be at the heart of the present conflict. In trying to negotiate with such a subject, you will find yourself alternating from questioner to statement maker; whenever possible, your statements should be affirmative or neutral. The purpose of your statements should be to clarify or to reinforce any positive gains made in the discussion and to present the subject with information that he may need to carry on with the discussion. As arbiter, you will have to set limits and define goals. Your authority as officer gives you this power, but you will want to be very careful about how you state those limits and goals.

For example, in the domestic dispute referred to above, you will be expected to set and maintain limits. During your questioning, you will undoubtedly have to interject statements defining what kind of behavior and actions are allowable and what are not. As the parties clarify their positions, you will have to be the one to define the gains made in the negotiation and define what still needs to be done. Your statements will serve as signposts for the continuing inquiry. At what might appear to be an impasse between the parties, for example, you might see the need for one subject to consider a new option. Therefore, you might say to one, "If you will lower your demand on this one point, I'm sure your wife would consider lowering hers on the other." Or, "You might not have as much trouble with this point if you first settle the other point." As mediator in any dispute, you have the responsibility to be alert to alternative approaches and options and be sensitive to the fact that each party in the dispute needs to feel confident that his or her interests are protected during any discussion of adjustment or modification. Any statements that you make, therefore, should be free of prejudice, as affirmative as possible, and forward-looking in the sense that by everything you say you project a sense of future adjustment and reconciliation.

During any arbitration in the street or in the home, you will have to be a shrewd *listener* — the third basic approach in determining purpose and assessing the needs of the people with whom you deal. Being a good listener involves more than merely *hearing* what another says; it involves *seeing into* what is heard. Remember the six "selves" present whenever two people sit down to talk (see Chap. 2): the "real selves" (two), the "self" as one sees oneself (two), and the "self" as seen by the other (two)? Listening is as much a persuasive tool as is speaking if we know how to listen, and the first thing we must keep in mind is that what one says can have several levels of meaning and can come from any one of the "three selves" mentioned above: the "real" self, the "self" as one conceives oneself, and the "self" as seen by another.

As a street officer, you know better than most that people often say one thing but mean another or they say one thing only to imply another. Moreover, subjects when confronted by officers will often initially attempt to "jive" them by appearing to be what they believe the officer wants them to be or by appearing to be other than they are. Distrust is a necessary habit of mind for the street-wise officer, for he knows that verbal misdirection is a way of life for many whom he confronts. Nevertheless, by skillful questioning, judicious statements, and intelligent listening, officers can see through such verbal misdirection and detect the real needs of their audience.

In making yourself a better listener, you must concentrate your attention on your subject's phrasing, his choice of expressions, his mannerisms of speech, and his voice or tone. You must also note and read his body language, his gestures of face and limb that provide clues to his real meanings and intentions. In trying to determine purpose, you are again engaged in audience analysis, for only by knowing your subject well can you know what must be done and how it ought to be handled. In any negotiation, changes in the psychological reaction of one party to another are marked as much by *how* something is said as by *what* is said, so you must be continually alert to subtle shifts in language or body movement. A shift from informal to formal language, for example, may be a clear indication that tension has suddenly increased in one of the subjects; a sudden crossing of the arms while talking may similarly indicate a hardening of position in the other subject. The examples are too numerous and complex to list, but in any discussion or verbal exchange you must attend carefully to the subtleties of changing diction, tone, and body language, as each can help you decide what course of action you must eventually take to resolve the present conflict.

From what has been said, it should be clear that to negotiate in the midst of heated controversy requires a fluid and flexible approach, a free and open mind. Disturbed and violent subjects usually are trapped in the *positional* bargaining game of attack and defense. You as the "third party" or disinterested instrument of society must change such frozen positions so that some kind of peaceful solution can be created. That is your basic purpose.

But though your purpose may never vary — you intend to quell a disturbance or to make an arrest — your approach to the achieving of that purpose can have a hundred variations and possibilities. A principle from ancient (and modern) warfare cautions the warrior to know when to abandon one set of means and attempt to win by another. Usually, that moment is when the warrior and his antagonist have become locked in battle to such an extent that no progress can be made by either. The modern equivalent of this is what Roger Fisher and William Ury call *positional bargaining* in their excellent book, *Getting to Yes: Negotiating Agreement without Giving In* (1981). They recommend that a negotiator try "negotiating jujitsu" and suggest that the arbiter attempt to deflect his adversary's energies into exploring the problem and inventing options for mutual gain (1981, p. 114).

For you the street officer, whether you are facing one adversary or attempting to adjudicate a dispute among many, your task by *job definition* is to orchestrate disinterestedly the extreme behaviors and perspectives of others. Like water altering its shape to fit its container, you must be malleable enough to change your approach as the situation dictates. Adaptation to circumstances is the fundamental principle of mastery. Avoid at all costs becoming "stuck" in one mode, one approach, for that is the behavior pattern of those you face. Moreover, if you don't, you become part of the problem rather than part of the solution. Your strength and power come from your ability to *shape* the situation to achieve your *ends*. Purpose and organization, therefore, are necessarily related and mutually dependent upon one another.

HOW TO DEAL WITH MULTIPLE PURPOSES IN ONE SCENE

To this point, we have examined only the relatively simple scene that contains one clear objective or purpose: the bar disturbance and the simple domestic dispute. But what about the more complicated situations in which purposes are multiple or where purposes *change* as the situation changes? In any police encounter, your purposes will be *legally* defined, *rhetorically* defined, or both. Police get calls because citizens believe some law or other has been broken or is about to be broken. Whether such is the case will be your job to determine. With your entrance into the scene, however, rhetorical considerations become important, and often these considerations can raise additional legal problems. Your initial purpose may become complicated by other potential purposes that are dictated by the exigencies of the rhetorical scene.

Consider the following example. Suppose you have been called to a residence because of a domestic dispute. The neighbors have called police because the couple carried their argument out into the yard. The time is late at night. You arrive and inform the couple that they are disturbing the peace, you request that they stay inside, and you do your best to settle the differences between the two. Thinking you have done this, you make no arrest. You leave. An hour later you are again called to the same residence, only this time the trouble has escalated. Neighbors tell you that they heard shouts and screams from the house and that they are concerned about the children's safety.

On again contacting the couple, you and your partner ascertain that indeed the argument has continued since your last departure. You are told the children are not involved, but you ask to see them to be sure. The children, a son and daughter, ages eight and ten, are brought down and seem frightened yet unmarred by the violence. The wife tells you that she fears for the safety of her children, but she will not sign a complaint against her husband. She is afraid of what he might do later. In your own estimation, the husband appears emotionally unstable, but he makes no threats towards you. Again you ask the wife if she wants to sign a complaint and she says no. The husband assures you that he will make no more trouble, but it is clear to you that by his sneer he means to make problems as soon as you are out the door.

What options do you have? Your initial purpose seems once again to have been temporarily gained; that is, the couple has stopped fighting and both assure you that they won't start it up again. But you and your partner are not convinced. The husband seems more than likely to carry on the argument, and you fear that if you have to return another time, some real violence may have been done either to the wife or to the children. Yet the wife will not sign a complaint, nor will the neighbors.

One option might be to take the approach that the two officers take in the case "Rhetoric as a Two-Edged Sword" given at the end of this chapter. In this case, the officers choose to use words to *stimulate* conflict between the violent husband and themselves. Using the device of side-commentary, these officers allow the subject to over-hear their negative comments about his manhood and he confronts the officers in rage and swings on one. The officers arrest him and take him to jail. The wife is absolved of the responsibility of getting her husband arrested, yet she and the children benefit from his absence.

In this instance, the officers work close to the line of police entrapment, but because they do not confront the subject directly — indeed, they hold their own private conversation — the subject remains responsible for his violent interference. The officers' actions and words precipitate violence, but it is for the greater good of the family. Such an instance illustrates the necessity for officers to be open and flexible in their approach and sure of the best purpose given the situation. Moreover, the case illustrates that purposes can change as the situation changes. Much of your success will depend on your ability to read a scene and to estimate accurately the present and the potential directions of conflict. Although it is true that police procedure may often dictate your purpose, as you have seen by this case illustration, just as often the situation itself will create new purposes to which you will have to respond.

The option taken in "Rhetoric as a Two-Edged Sword" should be regarded as a last-ditch effort. Other options in the present conflict illustration are several and probably should be tried first.

The strategic use of "the big threat" is one such possibility. This refers to the officers making what is essentially an unenforceable threat but one which works on some subjects, particularly on those who have something concrete to lose: prestige, pride, wife and children, material things, and status. In the present example, the two officers would tell the couple (equally, for rarely can an officer tell who is most at fault) that if they receive another call to that residence that night, one or both will be arrested. Pointing out that they do not have the time to keep returning to settle this one family's problems — indeed to do so would be a drastic interference in their ability to patrol their sector — the officers make it clear that an arrest will be their next and last option.

This option succeeds more often than not for three reasons: (1) most people do have something to lose by being arrested; (2) few people know the law well enough to know that a domestic dispute is not a crime; a social problem, yes, a crime, no; and (3) most people regard an officer's word as "law," and few want to take the chance that the officer cannot do what he says he has every intention of doing. The officer's ability to act convincing is crucial in such a strategy. Command presence, here marked by the officer's clarity of decision and confidence in his future action, usually creates in the subjects *belief* that the officer can and will do what he says. Again, the officer's role can create "reality."

Depending on an officer's professional assessment of the situation, two other options are possible in this domestic dispute: one stresses the ultimate purpose of separating the couple for a period of time; the other focuses on making the couple see the problem as a joint problem, a mutual problem-solving situation.

The underlying goal of all officers answering a domestic dispute is to settle the problem and get back into service. In the domestic problem we have been examining, one tack would be to separate the husband (or the wife if the officers feel that she might be easier to move) by offering to take him to a friend's house or to a restaurant for some coffee. By suggesting to the subject that perhaps all that is needed is to get away for a while, the officers may convince him to take their offer of a lift. In that case, the officers take the subject

where he wants to go and drop him off. It is important that the officers take the subject some distance away from home, for by the time
the subject has had his coffee and walked back, sufficient time to
cool off must have elapsed. This strategy prevents continuing conflict, provides a necessary period for cooling off, and avoids an adversary relationship between the couple and the officers. Several
purposes are thus accomplished by one strategy.

The final option goes even a step further in solving the immediate problem and in making the officers the "good guys" in the scene,
and of all the approaches, it is the most "civil" and the most psychological in orientation. It might be called "the counseling option" because the officers, in their second visit to the home, attempt to talk
the couple into allowing the officers to help them solve the problem.
Rather than threaten arrest or separate, they try to bring the couple
to the point where they will agree to shut down differences for the
night in exchange for the officers' aid in finding competent counseling services the next day.

Captain Bruce Fair, formerly of the San Jose Police Department
and now with the Emporia Police Department, tells me that such a
strategy is often employed in the big cities where there are crisis-
intervention services of considerable sophistication. Many of these
services, in fact, are free to the volunteers, and the street-wise patrol
officers know of them and use them often.

Whether the officers will be successful using this approach
usually depends on their rhetorical skill in convincing the couple that
they desire what is best for them as a family and that they are willing
to assist them in getting the aid they need. By assuring the couple
that they will contact them the following day with the needed information, the officers take a real step forward in establishing their
credibility with the couple, turning dispute into thought and creating an expectation of mutual problem solving.

This approach can be extremely useful with the chronic offender
on your beat as well as with the occasional problem family. A good
policy to follow with the chronic offending family is to notify the re-
ferral agency of the family's problems, thus increasing the likelihood
that some kind of contact will actually be made with the couple regardless of whether the couple takes the first step or not. The officer
who "backdoors" the couple in this manner does so for the couple's

good and for his own. His pragmatic concern is to smooth problem areas in his beat, and this "double-referral" serves as one way to accomplish this purpose.

From this extended illustration of a domestic dispute, we can draw several important observations about purpose and organization. Because a rhetorical scene is a dynamic thing, capable of changing and evolving in countless directions depending on the four elements of the situation — the exigency, the audience, the set of constraints, and the officers involved — purpose and structure will generally be highly problematic. The four strategies given here are similar in that the underlying, bottom-line purpose in each is to settle the dispute and get back into service. But each strategy is different from the others in the additional purposes that emerge from the particulars of the scene itself.

The severe option, maneuvering the subject into committing assault and battery on the officers, is based on the assumption that the officers have determined the subject to be beyond the bounds of reason and that the safety of the family is paramount. The purpose in this instance is to remove the subject for a sustained period of time while freeing the wife of all responsibility for the enforced separation.

The "big threat" approach, on the other hand, is based on the assumption that the officers have assessed the subject fully enough to count on his being cowed into compliance by their command presence. Their immediate purpose is to so dominate the subject (or wife if that should be the case) that they are capable of fully settling the dispute and getting back into service.

Both strategies involve an adversary relationship to the couple, to some degree or another. On the other hand, the advantages of the last two approaches lie in their non-adversary nature. The offer of aid in a temporary separation and the offer of future assistance in counseling both result in creating several positive goals. In each instance, officers work *with* the problem couple, not against them; in each, the officers create a situation wherein the subjects participate in the solution and the officers get back into service as efficiently as possible.

Although I have focused at length on a domestic problem, the basic strategies discussed can be applied in many other types of situations involving high tension and conflict, whether on the street corner, in a tavern, or some other such public place. Often, in fact, a scene may demand that two or more of these be used in sequence, and this is where the problem of organization and structure becomes primary.

Given a particular police call, the question you will always face is, what strategy to use first? Which second? Although it might appear that the more positive approaches should be tried first, it is not always so. Your ability to sift through conflicting stories and accounts and to judge for yourself the obvious and the not-so-obvious emotional tensions inherent in the scene will help guide your choices. So, too, will your judgment about the time you have to take with the call and other contributing factors, such as the time of day, the weather conditions, and the available resources at your command, help guide your eventual selection of purpose and approach.

Particularly useful in helping you decide on alternative approaches to a rhetorical problem are the Four Criteria that we discussed in Chapter 2. Remember, the four questions:

1. Is this option PRACTICAL?
2. Is it EFFICIENT?
3. Is it WORKABLE?
4. Is it consonant or consistent with other VALUES?

Had you faced the domestic situation described earlier, you could have made practical use of these questions to decide which of the four main alternatives was best in the given case. Because these questions address the problem of *means* to an *end,* they can serve as an informing tool of decision making. Seen from this point of view, then, the options presented in the domestic dispute are neither positive or negative in themselves but *situationally* good or bad depending on your analysis. Any decision that you make in the field should be based on as full a reading of the rhetorical situation as you can manage, given the constraints you find yourself working under.

STRUCTURING A SCENE TO ACHIEVE PURPOSE

Basic purposes in police work are identifiable. Officers most generally engage in:

1. Eliciting information from innocent citizens who have knowledge of a crime by virtue of being a victim, a witness, or other such probable source of information.
2. Confronting suspicious characters who may or may not be guilty of something.
3. Calming violent disturbances, in and out of the home.
4. Locating and arresting lawbreakers and traffic offenders.
5. Providing general assistance and aid as requested.
6. Disseminating useful information to the community on such topics as safe driving, drug and alcohol prevention, and home and business security.

Other purposes and duties exist, such as traffic control and maintaining a high degree of visibility, but the ones listed are those that typically call for a high degree of rhetorical skill.

Repeatedly, as you deal with the first four basic purposes, you will be faced with the problem of how best to structure or ORGANIZE your communication to achieve your end. Although you will always have to remain constantly alert to the possibility that you may have to switch approaches or strategies in the middle of the encounter, there are some fundamental principles that can help you organize your verbal discourse effectively.

First, learn to regard an encounter scene as a dramatic entity having a beginning, a middle, and an ending section. The initial contact (the beginning) with a subject is most vital, for if you miscue there, the rest will have little possibility of success. The best method for opening a verbal encounter with a citizen is to adopt a neutral and objective demeanor and voice. Generally, your task is to gather information and evaluate its worth; therefore, an open and flexible mind, together with a neutral to friendly demeanor, generates the best results. By definition, an opening is introductory, expository rather than persuasive, and your purpose is to discern the elements of the scene and to establish your authority and control over it.

Once your initial assessments of the elements and the problem have been made, you move into the *middle* part of the encounter. As part of your "move" or transition into this section, you adopt the appropriate role and position regarding the subject(s), including the most fitting voice and character that you deem necessary. This middle section is largely a matter of trial, error, and correction, and it is in this section that you employ the *strategies* of persuasion or behavior modification that you believe the situation demands. To do so, you must have determined in the *opening* section the purpose(s) you need to fulfill and remain alert to the possibility that these may change as the situation develops.

The middle section is best thought of as the *complication* section, as it is here that strategies may break down or new problems arise. Having established control in the opening, you must be very careful not to lose it in this section as new pressures or changes in purpose and intensity occur. The greatest mistake that you can make in this middle part of the street drama is to back a subject into a corner leaving him no way to escape with dignity. Many attacks on police result from leaving a subject no alternatives that he can see short of violent resistance.

The concept you must always keep in mind as you verbally interact with the people involved is that, like the movie or play director, it is your job to direct the energies and actions of the "players." Street scenes, as we noted earlier, change with your entrance into them and develop in the light of your handling of them. Like an actor, you must play the part that you selected in the opening and be prepared to change your script given a drastic change in scene. But like the director of the same movie, you must attempt to maintain structure and direction even when facing explosive and unforeseen turns of events.

To *end* an encounter successfully involves fulfilling your purpose and leaving those involved as well disposed toward you as you can reasonably manage. Giving citizens a "sense of an ending" is an important skill for shaping their impressions of you as a professional officer. Nothing hurts an officer's reputation as easily as his failure to create the sense of a satisfactory ending, given the law and the particulars of the rhetorical situation. Citizens who feel that you did not do an adequate investigation or inquiry, or who feel that your solution was hasty or somehow "unfair," leave a scene feeling hostile against you and the entire department. In some instances, such feeling is unavoidable (you can't please everyone), but the more often you can make even the unpopular decisions seem inescapable and legally (and morally) correct, the better your chances of creating respect for the work you have done.

The kind of "sense of an ending" that you provide partly depends on whether the scene that you have been handling is perceived by you as a one-time encounter or an encounter that may be the first of several future and continuing encounters. In the domestic dispute that we discussed at length, the option of separation and the option of "the big threat" presupposes a single encounter. The options each represent your belief that no further contact should be necessary. The possibility does exist that you may fail using these options, in which case further contact will be necessary, but you should act *as if* you expect these options to be sufficient.

The arrest option, on the other hand, may well result in continuing contacts with the family: the subject may return from jail only to pick up where he left off. The "counseling" option certainly presupposes further contact; indeed, you promise continued contact as part of the option. Your aim, then, will be to leave the family with the sense that you are helping them with their problem, not dissociating yourself from it.

Many typical encounters are of the continuing variety. Interviews with victims of crimes are of this sort, for often you have to recontact and maintain continuing communication. So, too, are the encounters with the repeating offender or the potential or real "snitches" who inhabit the street world. In terminating an encounter with such people, it is important to keep in mind the kind of relationship that you hope to perpetuate with these subjects over a period of time.

In all endings, it is important to see the situation from the other person's point of view. As in the typical car stop, no citizen will react as you do. You will forget the incident moments later, but the citizen will remember it with mixed feelings often for months. Your job requires you to interfere with the normal course of events in a citizen's life. The stop and frisk, the interrogation, the many recontacts all inconvenience people and often anger or embarrass them. The more you can appreciate this and anticipate it by the way you close an encounter, the more professional you will appear and the more effective you will be.

The first principle, then, entails seeing an encounter scene as a dramatic unity that you act in and direct to achieve your purpose.

Essentially *theoretical* in that it informs the way you see, it nevertheless has practical value because it allows you to impose order on what otherwise might appear random and disorderly and it keeps you alert to the evolving and dynamic nature of any verbal exchange.

The second principle is to use the law and departmental regulations to impose order on an encounter scene. Essentially *substantive* in nature in that it focuses on the materials that you have to work with, it nevertheless should, whenever possible, work in harmony with principle one. Simply stated, principle two is the "book approach" to street work. Some officers pride themselves on doing everything "by the book," an approach that encompasses both *stated* and *implied* laws, guidelines, and expectations.

Many of the ordering principles in the "book" pertain to the non-verbal areas of police work: how to handle a crime scene, how to conduct a high-speed chase in city traffic, or how to handle evacuation during a disaster. As street officer, you live in a world of defined procedures and expectations that aid you to achieve your purposes.

In the verbal areas, the rhetorical areas, the "book" can also be of some help. When you stop a suspected DWI (DUI) driver, there are several legal and departmental requirements that you use to pattern your investigation and arrest procedures. The law — here consisting partly of a legal definition of intoxication and partly on what you know to be the local court's requirements for conviction — helps you shape what steps to take and when. The crucial details that you look for, the number and kinds of coordination tests that you administer to the driver, and even the manner in which you handle the driver's vehicle, should he be arrested, are *all* influenced by the book. The book's value, then, lies in both indicating *what* can be done and, to some extent, *how* it must be done. It helps you structure, in other words, your means in achieving your purpose.

Your knowledge of the *law* and adherence to *police procedure* can also help you impose order on chaos in such scenes, for example, as major-felony calls. Suppose you have just received a call to break up a fight in progress in the rear of a tavern nearby. You arrive and discover that one of the persons involved is dead and the other has fled, leaving his jacket on the ground and his car in front of the tavern. The law and police procedure both necessitate certain steps, although the order of these steps may vary from department to department.

Your job as first officer on the scene is to call for backup, including a senior officer and the dicks. Almost immediately you know that you must seal off the area, which involves such precise steps as securing all clothing of the suspect and victim, securing the vehicle and sealing it, and keeping witnesses from leaving the scene. Additionally, as other officers arrive, you must distribute responsibility for some of these tasks among them. You know from departmental regulations that someone has to be in charge, which means you until the senior officer arrives.

A scene such as described is a potentially explosive arena, for, although the suspect has fled, typically there will be numerous individuals on the scene who are in emotional states ranging from shock to rage or who wish to disappear as quickly as possible now that you have arrived. Once you have determined that *your* safety is not threatened, you are able to proceed using the ordering patterns described; yet you are also unavoidably in a rhetorical situation and you must attempt to bring *principle one* and *principle two* into some kind of workable harmony. You have certain purposes that you must fulfil, but how you order those will depend on your reading of the dramatic scene that you confront.

To go by the book without a regard for the rhetorical exigencies or constraints is to be inflexible and ultimately inefficient. In any street encounter, you will want to consider the law, police regulations, and the rhetorical strategies appropriate to it. None of these, by itself, is sufficient. But all three, working in harmony, can help you define your purpose and order your actions in the most efficient and professional manner possible.

MINI-CASES ON PURPOSE AND ORGANIZATION

General Directions

Read each case twice to become familiar with the details, determine whether a case is a success or a failure, and then:

1. Determine the EXIGENCY in each.
2. List as precisely as you can the SET OF CONSTRAINTS present in the case.
3. Analyze the AUDIENCE in each. List crucial traits that the officer recognized or failed to recognize.
4. Describe the officer's initial PERSPECTIVE. Are his biases reflected in the way he handles the scene?
5. Is the officer clear on PURPOSE? Are there multiple purposes or one central one? Does the officer seem aware of purpose?
6. What strategies does the officer use to ORGANIZE his verbal communication to fit his audience? Does he make mistakes in shaping his discourse to the situation? If so, where? When does he begin to make errors? If he is successful, where does ORGANIZATION play an important part?
7. Define what laws are involved. What police procedures are involved? What demands issue from the rhetorical situation?
8. Consider the "larger implications" of the strategies used. Would the successful techniques pictured here *always* work? Sometimes fail?
9. Consider alternative approaches to the problem.

Case 1: "The Joe Duffy Episode"

Scene: At 2300 hours Officers Duffy and James respond to a fight call at Lindy's Tavern, 1100 Commercial Street. When they enter, it is crowded and noisy. The tavern owner motions them over to a corner booth where two college students are arguing.

Owner: Officers, these two guys have been pushing and arguing for ten minutes. This guy (points at Subject 1) just took a swing at that other guy (Subject 2) and I had to break it up. I want them out of here.

Subject 1: That's bullshit! I was just showing him what would happen to him if he wanted to step outside. But he's chickenshit! He called me an asshole and said I'd been bothering his chick. Hell, I was just talking to her! That's all.

Subject 2: Talking, hell! He had his arm around her and I heard him ask her to go outside. So I invited him out instead! But he doesn't like that scene as well.

Officer Duffy: Okay, okay, let's all step outside and talk about it there. We're not gonna get anywhere in here.

Subject 2: Not me! I haven't done nothing! I only protected what was mine. I don't need any hassles from you guys. Just take the asshole and leave me be!

Girl Friend: Yeah, leave him alone! You guys always pick on the wrong person. Just leave us alone!

Officer Duffy: Ma'am, we'll need to chat with you, too; now, outside! And, keep your opinions to yourself. I'm tired of hearing the same crap from you kids.

Girl Friend: Hey, I can say what I want! Now you're hassling *me!* Take a walk; we don't need it! And we don't deserve it!

2nd Woman: Hey, what's up? *(She has come from the crowd behind Duffy)* Duffy, what's your problem? Didn't you get enough last night from your old lady? Huh? Always taking it out on others, aren't you?

Officer Duffy: *(Turning to 2nd woman)* What, you here again? Drunk, too, huh? Sit down and have another. I don't need your bullshit; watch your mouth, lady.

Voice in Crowd: CRAM IT, OF-FI-CER! Back outta here, before you get hurt!

Officer Duffy: *(Turning around to face the crowd):* SHUT UP, JACK!

Officer James *(To Officer Duffy):* Hey, come on; let's get out of here; let's get these three out of here before the place blows.

Officer Duffy: Yeah, okay, but we don't have to take this kind of crap. Maybe we ought to clear the whole place and cool a few of these jerks at the station.

Subject 1: Yeah, terrific idea! Why don't you arrest everyone; that would sure make your night, wouldn't it?

Crowd: ARREST US ALL, ARREST US ALL. CLOSE THE PLACE! CLOSE THE TOWN! BIG MAN!

Officer James *(Takes hold of Subject 1):* Come on, let's talk outside. This is no good in here.

Subject 1: Okay, okay; it's too hot for me in here. I didn't want any trouble to start with!

Subject 2: BULLSHIT! First you make it hot, then you don't want any trouble. You're like Duffy here. You love trouble!

Officer Duffy *(Heading for Subject 2):* Okay, mouth, let's go. We're gonna have a little chat outside.

Tavern Owner *(To officers):* Hey, please guys; just get these guys out of here! It's not getting any better in here!

Officer James *(Seeing that the crowd is getting more and more pushy and loud):* I'm calling for some backup, Duffy. *(Takes his walkie and makes call)*

Scene: *One big guy stumbles into Duffy, pushed by someone in the crowd. Officer Duffy loses hold of Subject 2 and pushes student back into crowd. The crowd now surges forward, pinning the officers. The tavern owner yells at the crowd, but there is too much noise for anyone to hear him.*

Officer James *(He suddenly pushes several people out of his way and clears some space. He takes command.):* THAT'S ENOUGH! EVERYONE BACK! NOW! *(He pulls out his nightstick and the students step back.)* OKAY, EVERYONE BACK OFF NEAR THAT SIDE WALL. Now, you three out the door with Officer Duffy. NOW, THE REST OF YOU JUST COOL IT. *(He slowly backs out the door, following Duffy and the three subjects. Scene ends with officers backing out of the door and the sound of the backup officers.)*

Backup Officers: HEY, YOU GUYS NEED ANY MORE HELP? WHAT THE HELL HAPPENED?

Case 2: "Rhetoric as a Two-Edged Sword"

Scene: *Officers Fitch and Morse have had two prior calls to the same residence concerning a domestic dispute. In the first instance, husband and wife had been arguing and shoving each other when the of-*

ficers arrived, but neither one wished to file a complaint. The officers noticed that several pieces of furniture had been broken during the scuffle, and the couple's two children had fled upstairs upon the officers' arrival. The wife had claimed that the husband had threatened the children repeatedly, but that so far he had not hit them.

In the second call to the same residence, the wife claimed that she had been struck by the husband, and the officers could see several bruises on her cheek. She further claimed that he had twisted the arm of her smaller child, a boy aged six. But when officers asked if she wanted to file a complaint, she said "NO" — and she wouldn't go to her mother's home. She wanted to stay. The husband, also, refused to leave for the evening.

We pick up the officers in the third return call. They are knocking on the porch door. They can hear shouts and screams from within.

Officer Fitch: This is getting out of hand. We've got to do something this time. We can't be coming back here all night.

Officer Morse: That's for sure. This guy is becoming a danger to himself and others, don't you think?

Officer Fitch: Sure looks like it. Besides, we got other things to do than ride herd on these people.

Wife *(Opening door):* Oh, good, you're here again! This is getting too much. He has been beating me and he kicked Jason, my son, in the knee, twice!

Husband: COME OFF IT! It's none of their business, anyway. You're the one who's the problem! You slapped me, bitch, and I was only defending myself! *(Subject is shaking with anger and is barely able to talk)*

Officer Fitch *(To wife):* Well, want to sign a complaint now? We'll go with him; all you got to do is swear out a complaint.

Wife: Oh, no, you don't! You want I should be beaten when he gets out? Not me. I know his temper. He'll take it out on me and the kids. I ain't signing anything.

Officer Fitch *(Noticing the husband's self-satisfied smile):* Hey, come here a minute. *(He takes one of the husband's hands and looks at the knuckles)* I see you scraped your knuckles on something. How'd that happen?

Husband: Ah, you know. I work for a living. It must have happened at work.

Officer Morse: Is that why it's still bleeding? Did it at work, huh? Been bleeding for hours, huh?

Husband: Well, that's the way it happened. You don't like it? Tough! Prove otherwise!

Officer Fitch (*Aside, to Officer Morse*): Well, I guess big man here is tough on women and children. Remind you of something?

Officer Morse: Yeah, the guys in boot camp that couldn't make it. You know the type.

Husband (*Stepping forward, confronting both officers*): I heard part of that! Hey, this is *my* house! You calling me a coward? I've whipped tougher guys than you. (*He pushes Morse away and swings on Fitch. Fitch leans to one side, avoiding the blow, and takes the subject down. Morse helps.*)

Officer Fitch: You lose this one, big boy. (*They cuff subject and inform him that he is under arrest for assault and battery on a police officer. They read him his rights.*)

Officer Morse: We'll be going now, ma'am. He'll be spending the night with us. You can come down and bail him out in the morning.

Wife: Oh, I'm so sorry, officers. I didn't want him to go like this. (*Officer Morse takes husband out. Wife says to Officer Fitch*) Thank God! At least this way he won't blame me! He's been drinking heavy and maybe he'll be all right tomorrow. At least for tonight me and the kids can get some sleep. (*Scene ends as Officer Fitch continues to talk with wife.*)

Case 3: "Fingerprints"

Scene: *Officers Fitch and James are on routine patrol. They get a call to be on the lookout for a burglary suspect believed to be in the area. Tentative description: a white male, approximately six feet tall, 180 pounds. Last seen fleeing an apartment house; he is believed to be wearing a dark burgundy or brown T-shirt, jeans, and had been carrying a large grocery bag. Hair may be dark but color unknown.*

RP does not know if suspect has a vehicle. Last seen in the 1800 block of Lincoln.

Fitch: Hell of a deal! He's probably miles away by now. The RP waited fifteen minutes to call police.

James: Yeah; glad it's not our call. Let's cruise the general area. Maybe we'll hit on something.

Scene: *Several hours later, after numerous minor calls, the officers turn down a quiet residential street and notice a man apparently asleep in his car, head against the steering wheel.*

Fitch: Asleep at 10 PM, huh? Maybe he's passed out or sick. *(The officers pull up behind a dark green Chevy.)* Hey, the motor is still running. He's either keeping warm or he's out. Let's check it.

James: Sounds good to me. *(James raps on window with butt of flashlight)* Sir, sir, let's wake up in there!

Fitch *(To James):* Kinda looks like a dark T-shirt there, and jeans, too. Hard to say with his jean jacket, though.

James: Yeah, about the right size, too. I'll bet he's all of six feet or more. Let's get him out and have a little chat. *(Raps twice again on window with flashlight)*

Subject *(Sitting up and looking at officers):* Hey, what's the problem?

Fitch: Roll your window down, sir! *(Subject rolls window down)*

Subject: What's the hassle? I haven't done nothing. I'm just getting some shut-eye before I return to Hutchinson.

James *(To Fitch):* Call in and get any additional info on that other matter earlier. *(Fitch goes to patrol car. To Subject)* Just sleeping, huh. We thought maybe you were sick or passed out. Haven't been drinking tonight, have you?

Subject: Only a couple of beers, officer, and that was over an hour ago. Just leave me be!

James: Let's see some ID, please. We'll start with your driver's license.

Subject (Hands his DL out the window): Hey, look, I haven't committed any crimes by sleeping, have I? Just get off my back!

James: Please step out of your vehicle, sir. I detect a strong smell of alcohol in your car. You wouldn't mind doing a few field tests for me, would you?

Subject: Hey, it's cold out there! But I guess if you've got to have them before you stop hassling me, I'll do 'em!

Fitch *(Walking over to James and pulling him aside):* We may have something here. NCIC reports to be on the lookout for a subject with the same general description as this guy here; a three-state alarm. The sergeant says it would help if we got some prints off this guy. Last week Great Bend had a suspect with the same general description escape from custody. Sarge says if we get prints, we might match them to a set found in another case with a similar subject.

Scene: *Officers Fitch and James run subject through five field tests for DWI and subject passes all of them. NCIC shows NO RECORD for subject.*

James *(To Fitch):* We got problems now. This guy has ID, is not drunk, but he is edgy and did you note that load of paper bags on the floorboards?

Fitch: Yep. Let's jack with him a little. *(To subject)* What did you say you were doing in town, anyway?

Subject: Just seeing friends.

Fitch: All the way from Hutch to see friends, huh? Who were they?

Subject: Well, I never got to see 'em. They weren't home. They must have gone partying or something.

Fitch: Try some names, will you? *Who* did you come to see and *where* do they live?

Subject: Joe and Betty Samuels, but I'm not sure of their address. I may have gotten the wrong house.

Fitch: That's interesting. You got a phone number or an address?

Subject: Hey, I don't remember! I told you I couldn't find them. I had a phone number, but I left it back in Hutch.

Fitch: You don't know much, do you? You're just sitting in a car in a strange town having a nap, right? Down seeing people who don't seem to exist. Not too convincing. What about all those grocery bags in the back, there? You sell those, I suppose?

Subject: Hey, listen, Jack. I don't have to take all this crap! I've shown you my ID and I passed your crummy tests. Why don't you just shove off!

Fitch: Yeah, it's tough, isn't it? We've had some lizard burglarizing the neighborhoods around here and you kind of fit the description. You been filling your pockets with other people's stuff, Jack?

Subject: That does it! You got nothing on me! I'm leaving! *(Subject turns and opens his car door to get in)*

Fitch *(Keeps car door from opening all the way):* You don't mind if we search your car, do you, Jack?

Subject *(Pushes Fitch aside and tries to slam the door):* Take off, asshole. I'm within my rights. You got nothing!

Fitch: Sure we do, stupid. We got assault and battery on a police officer. You're under arrest. Now, GET OUT. *(Fitch pulls subject from car and cuffs him, reading his rights while doing so)*

James *(Looks through car):* Nope, nothing here but big grocery bags. If he had anything he must have hidden it elsewhere.

Fitch: That's okay. Let's roll with this jerk and take some prints while we're at it, whatcha say?

Scene: *Officers roll with subject. Subsequently, the subject's prints prove a match for those found in a burglary case in Great Bend. Under questioning, the subject admits that he had been involved in the apartment house burglary and several others in the area. He told officers where he had hidden the stuff he took that night.*

THE PROFESSIONAL PROFILE 7

*V*ERBAL JUDO has stressed the chameleon-like nature of police work: the ability to make oneself into what one must become to handle street encounters.

One underlying stress in this book has been that as a police officer, you are a professional partly because you are a knowledge worker who has to apply what you know under constantly varying and changing circumstances. Your ability to remain rhetorically flexible and shrewd in the face of tension and crisis is crucial to your safety and the safety of others. It is also what distinguishes you from the citizen; people call you because you possess the disinterest they lack. They need mediation. It is part of your professional profile.

So, too, is your "police perspective," the habit of seeing and reacting you develop from street experience. Like other professionals, you have a process of perceiving and responding to reality quite different from the outsider, the citizen. On the whole, such development is necessary and good; it is one of your strengths. It marks you as a pro, someone who knows how to deal with problems others cannot. You have a professional eye.

Yet, ironically, a latent danger exists in such perceptual development: you can lose yourself in your profession. Although your professional eye lets you see much that others can't, it also threatens to blind you to certain kinds of understanding, particularly the ability to see as others see. Surgeons forget what it's like to face an impeding operation, and lawyers forget the emotional trauma of testifying in court. Like these other professionals, you too can easily forget what it feels like to be stopped and questioned. In other words, professionalism, by its very nature, distances the practitioner from the non-practitioner.

One reason, then, that this book has argued for the rhetorical perspective, PAVPO, is that it insists that you never lose sight of the world as the other sees it. The acronym PAVPO reminds you, the practitioner, to see through the eyes of the subject, if only momentarily. A second value to PAVPO lies in its ability to help us "look harder" at an encounter. When we use it, it helps us not miss the necessary steps in scene analysis. It helps us be "ready."

But an acronym by itself is not inherently valuable; it is only valuable if you can make its meaning part of your automatic responses. One mark of your professionalism will be your ability to make the five rhetorical elements, PAVPO, part of your *system* of processing reality. PAVPO must become, in other words, part of your professional *struction,* not merely *instruction.* Consider, for example, another pro, the jet pilot. He habitually goes through a series of checks of his aircraft before he takes off; these "checks" are not written down — although they may have been in flight school — nor are they necessarily in the forefront of his consciousness. Automatically, almost unconsciously, he has internalized these steps. They have become part of his professional *struction.* PAVPO must become internalized in a similar manner; when this happens, you have turned instruction into *struction,* thereby streamlining your learning. Such streamlining makes for good spontaneous responses on the street. To possess this internalized process is another mark of the professional.

At this point we can say that as a police officer you share three criteria of professionalism with other professionals:

1. You are a knowledge worker who must apply your knowledge under constantly changing and varying circumstances.
2. You must be able to communicate effectively with those outside the profession.
3. You employ a process of action that requires *struction* as well as instruction.

But we know that being a police officer involves even more; it involves intense training in self-defense and weaponry. Along with your training in the law and police procedure, you receive hundreds of hours of instruction in the controlled use of force and firepower.

Verbal Judo has not addressed this part of your professional training, but a book on the use of words and verbal strategies cannot be complete without examining your professional necessity to occasionally use force. A full professional profile must suggest the proper blend of words and force.

The fourth criterion for professionalism is to know when to move from words to force. It is tempting to say that you should use force when your safety, or that of others, is directly threatened, for few would disagree. But the difficult question for the pro is, how can this necessity be determined? How can apparent threat be distinguished from real threat? One factor that makes police work so psychologically demanding is that there is no absolute answer to these questions. There is only probability. Such probability is determined by signs; one concrete sign of danger occurs when a subject couples aggressive *words* with *present ability*. A subject has present ability when he has the means and the opportunity to inflict injury. As a pro, you know that when a subject says he intends to hit you and he couples this verbal threat with an overt act, such as a lunge or some other violation of your private "space," you must be prepared to counter using force.

But situations are not always this clear. What about the subject who speaks non-aggressively while furtively reaching into his coat pocket? Here you face conflicting signs: words suggest one thing, but actions suggest another. Again you find yourself working in the area of probability. Depending on the general nature of the encounter, you will have to anticipate which to trust, but most experienced officers have learned to trust actions over words. A good street principle, then, might be stated like this: *when words and actions disagree, trust actions*. Although you must surely keep in mind that actions, too, can be misleading, whenever words and actions disagree you will be alert and ready to use force. This principle becomes part of your anticipatory mechanism that becomes internalized through repetition and experience.

You are *unlike* most other professionals in that you sometimes have to use force in the performance of your duty, but you are nevertheless *like* other professionals because when you make such responses you do so based on a professional process of decision making. You are not simply the victim of situation; you react according to internalized anticipatory patterns, patterns that have been shaped by training and past experience. Above all, these patterns are sensitive to your professional eye, your ability to read a scene for its latent danger. Hence, as a professional, your use of force will be both *selective* — you will know what kind of force and how much to use — and *appropriate* to your professional purpose. You will use force in a controlled, purposeful manner.

The amateur officer lacks such control. He uses force when he is personally challenged, or verbally abused, or feels he has lost face, or has tensions he wants to release. He will allow force to control him. Once he has used force, he will continue to think in terms of force. By contrast, the professional officer knows that even though he may have had to use force during a certain street encounter, he may *return* to words and verbal strategies once the threat to his safety (or that of others) is over. This ability to *return to words as soon as possible* is the fifth criterion of professionalism. The officer who can do this is working in harmony with the principles of common sense and rhetorical sensitivity.

The professional also can recognize "the special case," the subject who is reacting to drugs or to mental illness. Police departments are doing more than ever to train their officers in how to handle these special cases. For you on the street, it is imperative that you possess the knowledge to recognize by a subject's overt action that he is being compelled by some substance or some disorder out of the ordinary. Although you may still have to respond with force to such subjects in order to restrain them, you must act consciously in the knowledge of these special circumstances. Having possession of such knowledge, you will know what special steps you must take to apprehend, to restrain, and to provide assistance.

The seventh criterion for professionalism is the ability to *evaluate your own performance*. Like other professionals, you are constantly being appraised and evaluated by superiors. Precisely because police work is so rhetorical, so dependent on situation and audience, good evaluation is so difficult, particularly if the evaluator wasn't on the scene at the time. How many times, when you were negatively evaluated by a superior, did you find yourself thinking, "But he wasn't there; he can't know what it is like?" The typical police supervisors, from "the old Sarge" to the chief, have risen through the ranks. They have served their time on the street. But it is a fact that once a peer has risen to supervisory status, he ceases to be regarded by his former colleagues as a peer. He is different. He is "one of them," not "one of us."

The "old Sarge" ceases to be "one of us" because he wears a different pair of glasses; he finds himself concerned with new emphases: what the chief wants, what the public wants, what the statisticians want. Being held accountable by those above him, he now values accountability from those who work under him much more strongly. Good performance becomes defined as what he wants, what he thinks appropriate, and you find yourself thinking, "But he just doesn't know. . . ."

To be a professional you must be able to evaluate your own performance, both to yourself and to your supervisor. It first requires that you know why you did what you did in any given situation. You must develop the ability to be CONSCIOUSLY COMPETENT while you are performing so that later, in retrospect, you can review your actions intelligibly.

To be consciously aware of your own performance standards is a necessity. Professionals set their own criteria for good performance; they have that model in mind when they work. They keep that model constantly before them when they attempt an objective review of their performance after the fact. I suspect that much of the stress of police work, and perhaps a major cause of officer burnout, lies in an officer's inability to develop an appropriate and stable model for self-evaluation. The officer who repeatedly ends his day with questions that he finds he cannot successfully answer (Did I do the best I could given the situation? Did I have to use violence? Was there another way I could have handled the scene?) and who finds himself at the mercy of "the old Sarge's" estimates of the quality of his work is not going to last long as a professional. He must, like other professionals, learn to evaluate for himself the quality of his daily work.

Although every officer will have to develop his or her own performance model, let me suggest several criteria that ought to be part of such a model. First, use PAVPO to assess your work in review, as well as using it to guide your performance. Did you keep your *perspective* disinterested? Did you analyze your *audience* well? Did you adopt the proper *voice* to communicate? Did you keep *purpose* clearly in mind? Did you *organize* your communication and your handling of the scene as skillfully as possible, given the present constraints? Through such a review you will be able to assess your rhetorical skill in the scene that you are evaluating.

Another measuring rod might be to ask yourself whether you eliminated the *source of conflict* that occasioned the call. Was the problem taken care of, or will the subject or problem continue to be trouble for some other officer? For example, you may have made an arrest that was necessary, but you may have done it in such a fashion that the next officer to contact the subject or to go into the area will have a very difficult time of it. In solving one problem, you may have caused others. Another way of putting this question is, how much negative fallout did I cause because of the way I responded? If you caused none that you can see, you should feel that, at least from this perspective, you acted professionally.

In objectifying the quality of your work, especially in scenes in which you had to use some form of violence, you should ask, "Did I employ that force selectively and appropriately? Did I use the most suitable type of force? Did I use just what I need for the occasion, or did I become excessive?" As a professional, you should have responded according to those internalized patterns of anticipation that we mentioned earlier; analyze whether in fact you reacted to these or whether you became a victim of circumstances — something a pro never wants to have happen.

More important than my analysis at this point, however, is your own as you read these pages. Fill in your own criteria for your total professional model. Ask yourself, "What other criteria do I consciously or unconsciously believe are important for me as a police officer? In order to feel good about myself as a professional, what must I manifest, how must I act?"

I will close with one final observation about job performance, one I believe most clearly distinguishes the professional from the amateur. You must be capable of sharing your evaluation of your own job performance with your superiors. You must be capable of *describing and characterizing your performance.* To me, this is the sign of being fully CONSCIOUSLY COMPETENT. Not only must you be able to describe what you did and why, but you should be able to show that what you did was based on a principle of professional action, on the *struction* you have developed as a street officer. Amateurs at best are UNCONSCIOUSLY COMPETENT. That is, they may respond well to a given situation, but they will not be able to describe why they acted the way they did. Their successes are often chance and accident. A professional, by contrast, will be able to *describe* what he did and *characterize* his actions as part of a larger, more definable pattern of behavior. This is the full meaning of the phrase CONSCIOUSLY COMPETENT.

Your total professional profile, then, involves knowing how to use words skillfully and how to employ force selectively. By way of summary, a list of the major criteria of professionalism follows, but you must complete the profile for yourself. Although most citizens do now know (or do not appreciate) how fully professional police officers can be, you as the individual police officer must know. You must know for your own continued growth in the profession, and you should be able to define to others what it is you do and why you are proud to do it. In this way, not only will your department attract better and better recruits, but the message of your professionalism will gradually become understood and accepted by society at large. To move in such directions can only make society a safer and a more civil world in which to live.

A Checklist for the Professional Officer

- Professional officers apply knowledge under changing and varying circumstances.
- Professional officers communicate effectively with those outside the profession (PAVPO).
- Professional officers employ a process of action that relies on *struction* as well as *instruction*.
- Professional officers know when to move from words to force.
- Professional officers employ force both *selectively* and *appropriately* because they react according to an internalized process of decision making.
- Professional officers know that even if they have had to use force, they can return to the use of words as soon as possible.
- Professional officers can recognize the "special cases" where

subjects are driven beyond their control by mental illness or controlled substances.

- Professional officers can evaluate their own performance.
- Professional officers are capable of describing and characterizing their performance to their superiors.

BIBLIOGRAPHY

Bavoka, William H.: *Training in Depth Interviewing.* New York: Harper and Row, 1971.

Benedetti, Robert L.: *The Actor at Work.* Englewood Cliffs, N.J.: Prentice – Hall, Inc., 1976.

Corbett, Edward P.T.: *Classical Rhetoric for the Modern Student.* New York: Oxford University Press, 1965.

Fisher, Roger; and Ury, William: *Getting to Yes: Negotiating Agreement without Giving In.* Boston: Houghton Mifflin Co., 1981.

Flower, Linda: *Problem-Solving Strategies for Writing.* New York: Harcourt, Brace, Jovanovitch, Inc., 1981.

Glenn, Stanley L.: *The Complete Actor.* Boston: Allyn and Bacon, Inc., 1977.

Hairston, Maxine: *A Contemporary Rhetoric,* 3rd ed. Boston: Houghton Mifflin Co., 1982.

Hyams, Joe: *Zen in the Martial Arts.* New York: Bantam Books, 1982.

Maanen, John Van: "The asshole." In Manning, Peter N., and Van Maanen, John (Eds.): *Policing: A View from the Street.* Santa Monica, Calif.: Goodyear Publishing Co., Inc., 1978, pp. 221 – 237.

Manning, Peter K., and Van Maanen, John (Eds.): *Policing: A View from the Street.* Santa Monica, Calif.: Goodyear Publishing Co., Inc., 1978.

Mischel, Theodore: *Understanding Other Persons.* New Jersey: Rowman and Littlefield, 1974.

Muir, William Ker, Jr.: *Police: Street Corner Politicians.* Chicago: University of Chicago Press, 1977.

Musashi, Miyanto: *The Book of Five Rings.* New York: Bantam Books, 1982.

Nierenberg, Gerard I.: *The Art of Negotiating.* New York: Hawthorn Books, Inc., 1968.

Nierenberg, Gerard I., and Calero, Henry H.: *How to Read a Person like a Book.* New York: Hawthorn Books, Inc., 1971.

Rogers, Carl: *Freedom to Learn.* Columbus, Ohio: Charles E. Merrill Publishing Co., 1969.

Robbins, Stephan: *Managing Organizational Conflict: A Non-Traditional Approach.* Englewood Cliffs, N.J.: Prentice – Hall, Inc., 1974.

Schelling, Thomas C.: *The Strategy of Conflict.* Cambridge, Mass.: Harvard University Press, 1960.

Young, Richard E., Becker, Alton L., and Pike, Kenneth: *Rhetoric: Discovery and Change*. New York: Harcourt Brace, and World, Inc., 1970.

Watson, Nelson A.: *Issues in Human Relations*. Gaithersburg, Md.: International Association of Chiefs of Police, 1973.

Zartman, William I.: *The 50% Solution*. Garden City, N.Y.: Anchor Press/ Doubleday, 1976.